QUEST

My Journey Through La Mancha

DAVID LANGE

RED
PENGUIN
Books

Quest: My Journey Through La Mancha

Copyright © 2020 by David Lange

This book has been approved for public release by the Department of Defense, Defense Office of Prepublication and Security Review.

The views expressed in this publication are those of the author and do not necessarily reflect the official policy or position of the Department of Defense or the U.S. government.

Published by Red Penguin Books

Bellerose Village, New York

Library of Congress Control Number: 2020913939

ISBN

Print 978-1-952859-13-7

Digital 978-1-952859-21-2

CONTENTS

For Valerie
... and for all those who inspire and make this world a better place
through their caring and compassion

With special thanks to Dorothy
... and to all the dreamers who struggle but refuse to give up

When hope is lost . . . hope.

FOREWORD

There are countless ways I can tell my story. Above all, I wish to tell it truthfully; but first I must set the stage, and I do so thusly...

I stood alone where the sea met the land, and I turned to survey the path that had taken me here. Despair. Glowing embers were all that remained. Time had stolen my childhood joys and burdened me with an unwelcoming and uncaring existence. There was no going back. I knew this, yet I strained to see if I might find something to unite me with my lost happiness. Smoke obscured my view. I turned to the sea. The sea was vast and unknown; the sky above dark and foreboding. The water formed an impassable barrier. Unable to retrace my steps and incapable of continuing across the water—I was trapped—a prisoner. I had no reason to hope for better.

I did not pray. I did not ask for help. I did the only thing I could do—I prepared myself for the end and resolved to face it stoically. This was enough. I was no longer afraid to die alone and unsung. I would leave this world honorably and without regret. I was ready.

A thick fog rolled in off the sea, like the smoky breath of some great beast, and obscured all in its path. My eyes strained to see beyond the shadowy curtain. The wind subsided and the waters were eerily still. Then I felt something stirring within me—a feeling I had never before known. I had no words to describe it. I had no idea what it meant. It was different; and, on this day, different was welcome.

In the distance, I detected movement at the outermost limit of my mist-enshrouded world. From the sea, a shadowy apparition approached. Was this to be my fate? Was I to be devoured by some unholy creature after having been driven from my homeland? This was no worse than the alternatives I had envisioned. As the specter drew nearer, I saw that it was no beast but rather a boat with a dragon's head carved at the bow. The strange craft, devoid of any crew, drifted to the shoreline and settled there for consideration.

Life presents us with choices. We may never know the forces that drive us towards these options, and we will rarely know the outcomes of our decisions beforehand. Some have said that fortune favors the bold. Others proclaim that safety and success are best realized by traveling familiar roads. The most prudent travelers logically evaluate each decision in the context of their current situation and desired outcomes. But then there's that odd lot, a unique brand of individuals, that look for signs and portents —they blindly follow their heart, convinced that the path they follow must necessarily be preordained by destiny or prescribed by the Heavens.

A dragon boat mysteriously emerges from the fog and drifts towards the shore where it settles. Our choice reflects who we truly are. Do you climb on board? I made my choice in 1982. My adventures would take me across the globe. I would fight in two wars, and I would also contribute to saving countless lives. I would surmount great peaks of joy and struggle through dark swamps of despair. I would doubt myself time and time again yet I would not surrender. When hope seemed lost, I was blessed by miraculous happenings that defied anything my rational mind could account for. In a world that drives us towards conformity, I was unrelenting in my efforts to retain my individuality and to always be uniquely me. When I look back upon all of this, I remember...I remember Valerie, dear Lady Valerie. I am grateful.

Chapter One

MY LAST CHANCE

*B*aseball hat—check. Watch—check. Jacket—check. It was July 31, 1982. I was 15 years old; and I was running through my packing checklist for our upcoming trip to Portugal, Spain, and Morocco. The door was closed to my small room, decorated much as it was when we moved to the house in 1971—blue walls with nautical wallpaper trim along the upper border and one solid wall wallpapered with a distinct nautical theme—a boy's room. It was quite warm; but fortunately, the unusually cool weather of the past week had made the days preceding our vacation unusually pleasant. This was a welcome contrast from the hot and muggy summer days I was accustomed to. Our home's single wall-unit air conditioner, located in the living room, did little to cool the bedrooms around the perimeter on the lower floor of our 1950-built ranch-style home in Great Neck. My room, the smallest bedroom in the house, had only one small exterior wall. As such, my living space was admirably warm during the winter but, unfortunately, stifling hot during the summer months. With my friends away for the summer, July and August were typically hot, boring, and somewhat lonely. Still, I welcomed the break from school and the opportunity for some unstructured time to play and to reflect upon life. Regrettably, my reflections had long since turned to brooding. Unhappy thoughts began to cloud my mind. It was a challenging time in my life, and several external factors had added to my growing teen angst creating a general state of despair and self-doubt. I felt my life was spiraling out of control, and I no longer liked who I was nor saw any hope for redemption. I was a passenger on a runaway train and desperately hoped for anything that might lift me out of this emotional morass.

I was not typically enthused about our summer family vacations, but I did harbor a small bit of hope that the upcoming trip might provide some level of inspiration or at least lead to some change in my mental state. My interest in the opposite sex was only just developing; and there was a part of me that was hopeful I might find a girlfriend although I knew this would be unlikely since I was traveling with my mother, father, and younger sister. In the end, I'm not sure what I was looking for; but I was definitely looking for something. I had a strange feeling inside that this was my last chance—my last chance to turn my life around and my last chance to save myself.

I continued packing my carry-on bag and checking items off my checklist until all 30 items were accounted for. I was quite the organized teen. In an unsure and increasingly complicated world, my organizational projects provided a pleasant retreat. I was putting my life in order on a very small scale. This was comforting considering I felt little control over any other aspect of my existence. This year I added a new item to my checklist—a trip log. I was interested to see how this experiment would pan out. While I was not one for diaries or journals, I decided I would document all the events of the upcoming vacation. There would be little in the way of commentary—the log would describe places visited along with a precise timeline of events. I can't remember now why I decided to create the trip log for this vacation, but it proved fortuitous that I did.

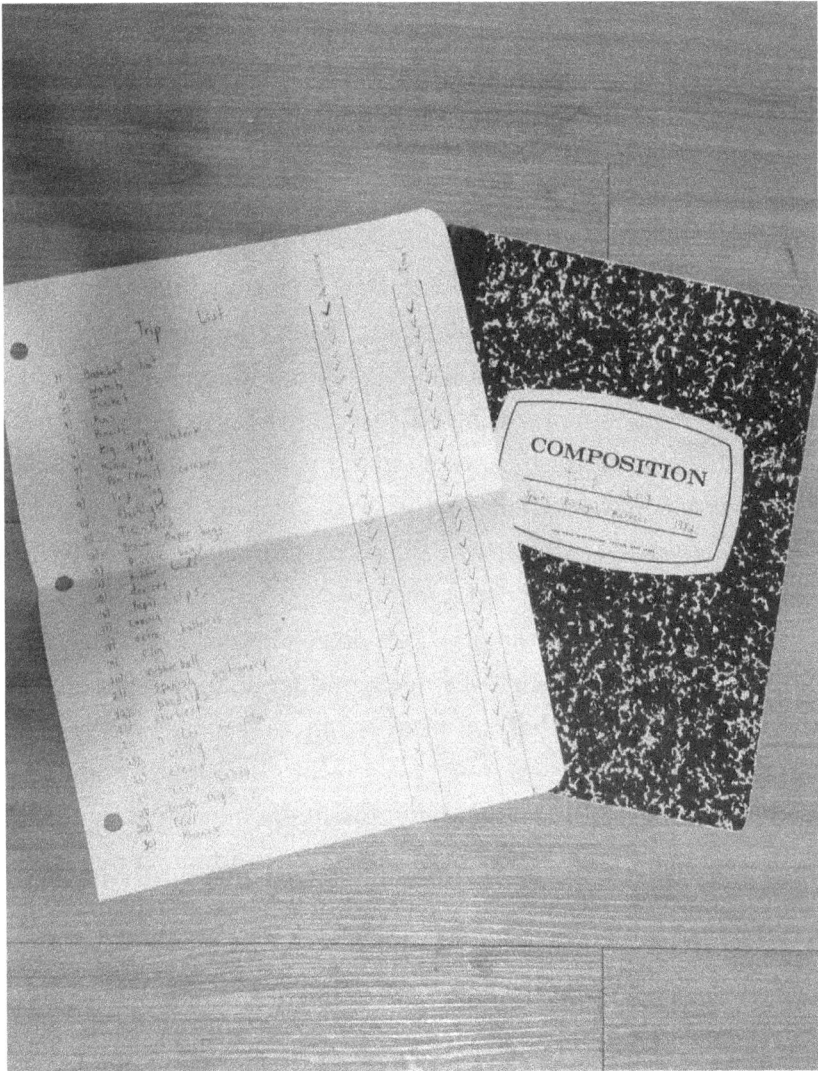

Trip Log and Packing List for 1982 summer vacation

On this last night of July, I changed into my pajamas, said good night to my parents, partially closed my door, and tried to get to sleep. With so much on my mind, sleep did not come easily. Eventually, my eyelids closed and July slipped away as unremarkably as it had arrived. I had little reason to believe that August would be any different. I was wrong. The first day of August was to be the first day of the rest of my life. Events were already set in motion as I lay asleep that night. If a young man's wish holds the same power as a heartfelt prayer, then perhaps someone, somewhere, heard me.

I was deliberately raised without any religion; and I was not one to pray or ask for help from God, but I was also a spiritual person. As unfocused as it may have been, I had faith that there was more to the world than what my eyes and senses revealed to me. I believed in something—I just didn't know what. I knew better than to ask for or expect anything, but my common-sense practicality could not deny me the small grains of hope that every child keeps within his heart. I didn't think that August would bring any relief. I hoped that it might.

I don't recall what time I awoke on August 1st. I do recall that the day had a single focus—I would conduct final preparations for the trip. I regretted that my brother, once again, elected not to travel with us. John was not only my brother; he was my best friend in this world. Additionally, his fluency in Spanish would have been a great asset on this vacation. Unfortunately, after traveling abroad with us only twice, my brother had concluded that he did not fit the tourist mold. He didn't wish to look upon poverty and a troubled world through the lens of a tourist camera, and I can't deny that I've felt similar guilt upon occasion. My brother was ten years older than me, and I respected him so much that I never questioned his decision. My traveling buddy, this trip, would be my sister, Jennifer. Only two years younger, Jenny and I generally got along very well and, especially on vacation, closely bonded and shared countless inside jokes. As on previous trips, Dad and I would be travel partners and share a room while Jennifer and Mom would team up. Everything was in order when the Ollie's Airport Service van arrived at our home at 3:45 pm on that Sunday afternoon. It was sunny and a pleasant 81°F as we loaded our two suitcases and four carry-on bags into the van with the help of the driver. As we pulled away, I turned for a final glance back at our house. This was our 6th trip abroad, and I knew I'd be missing home soon enough. I definitely had mixed feelings. I was interested but certainly not excited. All the same, I was ready for the adventure to begin.

As it was Sunday afternoon, the traffic was relatively light as we made our way to John F. Kennedy International Airport. The trip took just over thirty minutes. After arriving at the airport, we carried our bags over to the TWA check-in counter and took care of all the normal pre-flight business.

I've always found airports to be exciting places. The fact that I rarely had the opportunity to visit them added to the mystique. International airports, especially, are fascinating crossroads of the world. Beyond admiring the hustle and bustle of the scene, I was also on high alert for, shall we say, possibilities. As we headed to our gate in the International Terminal, my "scanning radar" was up and fully operational. There's no denying it, I was on the lookout for any girls of interest who might possibly be on our trip. Previous vacations seemed disproportionately populated with middle-age to elderly New Yorkers, and I didn't have any expectation that this trip would be different. However, it never hurt to keep my eyes open. While I was, and am still, proud to be a New Yorker, I found that my fellow travelers were often aggressive and ill-tempered vacationers, more so when unleashed within the fast-paced, minimum-sleep, lower-end tours we had frequently taken.

Our first few "International Weekend" vacations were typical of this rat-race. The memories still make me cringe—tourists constantly fighting for window seats on the bus and complaining at every inconvenience. The year prior was a notable exception—a spectacular trip to England and Scotland with our initial leg taken upon the Queen Elizabeth 2 ocean liner. I was fairly confident that this American Express Iberian Sunseeker tour would fall short of that mark. Still, with several years of Spanish under my belt, I was interested in the culture and in seeing the famous castles of Spain. However, with little say over the agenda, I was expecting to see more cathedrals than castles. Visiting any church with my father was a very uneasy experience. I knew better than to ask any questions or ever start up a conversation about faith or religion. At "holy places" my father's intensity and discomfort could not help but permeate the family. While I was impressed with the larger medieval cathedrals, I must admit that I could not wait to get back into the fresh air and on to other sites of interest (and less emotional drama).

At 6:50 pm we boarded TWA Flight 900, a Lockheed L-1011 Tristar bound for Lisbon, Portugal. I was still searching for possible members of our group. After all, they'd all be coming from New York, right? I had only taken my first airplane flight five years earlier, in 1977, so I was still extremely excited about getting to fly. The acceleration of takeoff, especially, was a thrill for me. At 7:45 pm, we were off. New York faded below as we turned towards the ocean on an eastbound heading. The flight was scheduled for about 6.5 hours so we all settled in. We were served a snack at 8:40 pm and then struggled through the turbulence to put away our dinner at 10:20 pm. The feeding schedule was completely out of sync with our usual dining hours. Following our inflight dinner was a fruitless attempt to grab some brief moments of sleep before our final landing in Lisbon at 6:24 am (Lisbon time). The lost night of sleep combined with the five-hour time change would put us all off our daily rhythm for days to come. The first day of the month expired somewhere over the vastness of the Atlantic Ocean. It was now August 2, 1982, a day I commemorate every year. It was the first day of the rest of my life.

Chapter Two

ENTER DULCINEA

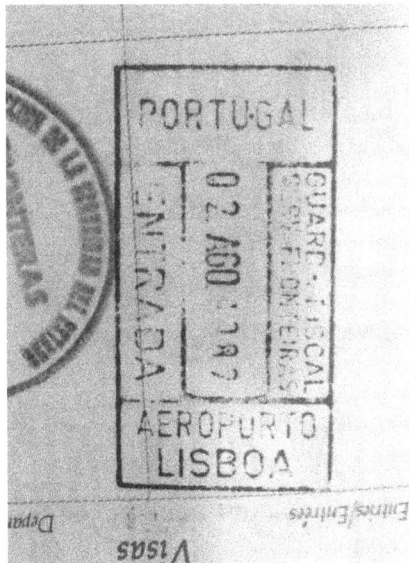

Passport entry stamp, Lisbon, Portugal (August 2, 1982)

*L*anding in Lisbon, our brains were all in a fog. As best we could, we prepared ourselves for the challenges of clearing through Customs, recovering our baggage, and getting linked up with our tour group at the airport. Unfortunately, this time it was more difficult than on previous trips. There were no banners, no tour guides yelling our tour name or waving a company flag, and no one advising us where to go. We followed the crowd and, eventually, managed to find our tour group and our bus. The hard part was done. While on the short bus ride to our hotel, I quickly scanned the members of the group to see if anyone caught my interest. No luck. However, I was quite tired so my efforts were only half-hearted. There would be other opportunities. We arrived at the Hotel Diplomático just after 8:00 am, checked in, put our luggage in our rooms, grabbed a quick snack in the hotel coffee shop, and then returned to our rooms for some much-needed sleep. I could not have known at the time that the most special member of our tour group had arrived earlier, traveling not from New York but from Italy where she was visiting friends. As such, my initial assessment of the situation left little room for either inspiration or hope. Of course, none of this mattered much as I drifted off to sleep at half-past 9:00 am, napping all the way through to 3:00 pm.

In a state of consciousness that barely qualified as being awake, Dad, Mom, Jen, and I went out looking for something to eat. We came upon a small department store with a snack bar and got some simple sandwiches to carry us over until the dinner event later that evening. We also visited a book store where I stumbled upon a book I really liked. However, since it was written all in Portuguese, this presented a bit of a problem. I jotted down the name, *The Rand McNally Color Illustrated Guide to Sailing Ships*, and resolved to seek out this book when I returned to the States. In the pre-internet days of 1982, that would be no easy task. Nearly two decades later, the book, in English, would finally be mine.

After our snack, we returned to our hotel rooms and rested again, between 5:40 pm and 7:30 pm. The first official event of our tour was to be a dinner with live entertainment at Machado's Restaurant. I can't say that I was really looking forward to the experience. For starters, I was still feeling quite exhausted. The nap had done little to readjust my body for any kind of normal operation. And, more importantly, my parents insisted I wear a nice jacket and tie to the dinner. I found this greatly troubling. I was a windbreaker and baseball cap kind of guy, and I felt that these "fancy clothes" were not only contrary to my style but also, and more to the point, another attempt at bullying me into "selling out." Of course, as a 15-year old, my protests were somewhat limited; although I did have some additional leverage after the Batu Caves disaster of several years prior. That, however, is a different story. I will state simply that, after the most vicious parental attack of my life, in a desperate effort to get me to part with my windbreaker, the greatest storm set upon this earth since the Great Flood, and a storm not at all in any forecast, ended a years-long assault upon my fashion choices and put an end, once and for all, to my parent's attempts to get me to part with my jacket. There is no doubt my experience in 1979 at Malaysia's Batu Caves was still very fresh in my mind on this second day of August in 1982.

Our tour group met in the hotel lobby at 8:30 pm and boarded a large touring bus. I was exhausted. Our tour guide, Ms. Maria Malta, introduced herself. Our guide requested that when she called our name off the trip roster, the leading member of each party should stand and say where they were from. We went through this exercise as the bus traveled to the restaurant. For the most part, the names seemed pretty standard; and the residences, likewise, were mostly New York or East Coast locations. "The Langes," said our tour guide. My father stood up and replied, "New York." And on it went. Then, our tour guide called out, "Ms. Dudoward." From the row immediately in front of my father and me, a young woman stood up and, with a very gentle voice, replied, "Canada." Well, this got everyone's attention, including my own. The bus was dark and I could not see her very well, especially since we were directly behind her; but she seemed to be an attractive young woman and I imagined her to be somewhere in her mid-twenties. The fact that we had a fellow tour member from a different country generated a fair amount of side conversation amidst the tourists. I had always liked Canada and thought well of Canadians so I definitely felt that this was a good omen. We finished introductions before the bus arrived at Machado's, just before 9:00 pm.

If my brain was trying to determine whether it should be waking up or going to sleep, my stomach was likewise confused. A late dinner, 9:00 pm to 11:25 pm, was not normal for my family, in any time zone. I remember little about the food other than being hungry, enjoying the bread and water, and finding myself pleasantly surprised with some stuffed clams that exceeded my expectations for anything so unusual sounding. I was a hamburger, hot dog, pizza kind of kid and this unusual fare was very risky. The lights of the restaurant were very dim; and a spotlight highlighted the area where various performers played their instruments, sang, and danced. I'm sure the performances were fine, but my brain hurt too much to focus. I literally hunched over in my seat, occasionally closing my stinging eyes to relieve the painful irritation. We were treated to traditional Portuguese Fado music which, by its nature, tended to be a little bit sad. I don't know whether or not it was the music, the exhaustion, or something else that caused my mind to drift to strange places and for strange feelings to fill my heart. I did, occasionally, look over to where our Canadian companion was sitting. It was too dark to see much. She was very pretty. On this night, however, my eyes strayed elsewhere—to a portrait on the wall that I can describe as nothing less than haunting. It was a sketch of a very beautiful woman whose expression struck me as being very sad. I'm not sure what it was about that picture, but it pulled me in and I became totally entranced. I could think of little else besides that picture. I wondered who this beautiful woman was and contemplated why she might look so sad. I felt an incredibly strong desire to help her. I desperately wished that I could save her from whatever misery or woe was troubling her. I stared, and stared, and stared. When the dinner was over, I returned to our awaiting bus with the group...but that portrait never left my mind. We got back to the hotel at 11:40 pm and were in bed, finally, at 12:15 am. I don't know that I slept more than a few hours that night, but I do recall thinking of little else besides the woman in the portrait at Machado's. At the time, I did not place any special significance upon this fascination; but looking back, years later, I have to think that something was happening deep inside of me. I don't fully understand what it was, but the stage was being set for a change in my life and I never saw it coming. It was wrong that a woman should be sad, and I cursed the causes of such misery. If only there were a hero to take away the pain. This world needs a few more heroes. I was not a hero. I was nothing like a hero. Heroes are born of passion and courage. Many thoughts raced through my brain; and with the never-ending flow of traffic circulating below and my mind completely occupied, I was unable to sleep. Morning came, all the same; and before I knew it, my father's alarm was ringing at 7:30 am on August 3rd.

Dinner at Machado's Restaurant (August 2, 1982). My family is at the right. Defiantly, I refuse to look towards the camera.

Our group had one goal for the 3rd of August, a city tour of Lisbon. It's really quite amazing that I was able to drag myself out of bed and to breakfast at the hotel that morning. Twenty minutes for eating, a quick clean up, and we were on the bus at 9:00 am. I was still in such a daze that I don't recall many elements of the tour other than getting to spend some time at the Castelo de São Jorge, at least one old church, and the Monument to the Discoveries. I liked Lisbon, and the weather was pleasantly cool with a nice sea breeze coming in. Sadly, the beauty of Lisbon could not resuscitate my body; and I struggled to stay awake as we drove through the city, admiring the attractions and listening to stories of the city's history. We returned to our hotel shortly after 1:00 pm and ate lunch in the hotel's restaurant. It probably comes as no surprise that my family adjourned to our rooms after lunch and napped for about three hours prior to getting up to do some more independent exploring around the local area. We looked at the shops, returned to the hotel, ate dinner, and went to bed.

Cannon at Castelo de São Jorge, Lisbon, Portugal

August 4th was even less inspiring. We woke up at 6:30 am, ate breakfast just after 7:00 am, and were on the bus for an all-day ride towards Seville at 7:55 am. The day can be summed up by endless driving interspersed with the occasional comfort break or meal stop. We incurred another one-hour time change, just to add insult to injury. I tried to catch up on my sleep during the road trip but likely would have served my body better had I fought to stay awake and forced my body into a more normal sleep cycle. Regardless, the long road trip came and went and we pulled into the Hotel Macarena in Seville at 6:50 pm. We ate dinner at 8:00 pm and our group later gathered to head to a Flamenco show at El Patio Sevillano. I don't recall seeing "the Canadian Lady," as I now referred to her, at the show. What I do recall is an embarrassing moment with my family—the kind that all teens dread. As the waiter came to take drink orders, my Dad told him that the children would both like a Coke. We continued to enjoy the music and dancing while we awaited our complimentary drinks. When our drinks arrived, it was pretty clear to me that this was no ordinary Coca-Cola. The waiter had, in fact, brought me and my younger sister two rum-and-cokes. Dad was not pleased. Since I was a student in Spanish, Dad asked me how someone would say "it's terrible." I gave him a few options. He then asked how one would say "no more" and I responded with the classic "no más." I honestly didn't think Dad was planning to actually make use of his newly acquired vocabulary, but he cut loose with a very intense combo when the poor waiter came to visit. I don't believe we ever did get replacement beverages, but there was no doubt the waiter wasn't going to bring us any more rum-and-cokes. I felt so embarrassed. The show ended at 11:00 pm; and after the ride back, we were calling it a night just prior to midnight. It was another long day and I was exhausted.

Chapter Three

QUIXOTE IS BORN

ugust 5th and things were different. My energy was back and, after a good night's sleep, I was operating at about 75% capacity. The day began normally enough—up at 7:30 am, breakfast in the hotel at 8:20 am, and on our tour bus for a city tour of Seville at 9:30 am. There wasn't anything else normal about this 5th day of August. To this day, I cannot explain in words how abruptly and how deeply I fell in love—but I did. She was beautiful. Valerie was beautiful...absolutely beautiful. Illuminated like some angel beneath the brilliant glow of the Spanish sun, Valerie looked breathtakingly lovely. That day she wore a light, summery, single-piece purple jumper that was at the same time classy and cool. The lower half of the outfit tapered modestly to a short cut leg. Valerie had a lovely tan and a great figure, but what I noticed most and remember best was her lovely smile. Everything about her was amazing—from the way she gracefully moved about to the gentle tones of her sweet voice. I was literally entranced and could not keep my eyes off of her although I fought the urge as best I could. That day we saw beautiful cathedrals, the

Plaza de Toros, the Torre del Oro, and countless other sights. I saw only Valerie. I felt a desperate need to maintain proximity yet when we would stop to look at things along the tour, I would virtually freeze and my heart would race whenever I was near her. I had absolutely no idea what was going on inside my head—but it felt wonderful. At this point in the tour, I still didn't know her first name nor did I know anything about her. As we strolled across the beautiful Plaza de España, my mind wandered dreamily; and I felt a strange sense of peace amidst the confusion. There was no doubt about it—I was falling in love.

Valerie was the type of wonderful person that inspired acts of chivalry. I wanted so very much to do things for her, to be a gentleman, to find some subtle way of saying "you're amazing." At stops along the way, I would purposefully time my arrival back at the bus to match Valerie's arrival. At times, I'd walk ridiculously slow while, at others, I'd virtually race to arrive at our tour bus simultaneously so that I might politely permit Valerie to enter first. Ladies first. This was chivalry, in my love-enthralled mind. This all seems somewhat crazy now, but love and adoration can drive a man to depart from normal standards of conduct and behavior. My chivalrous attempts, as poorly conceived as they may have been, would continue through the remainder of our tour.

Valerie Dudoward, Spain (August, 1982)

We returned to our hotel at 1:33 pm and had lunch in the hotel before adjourning back to our room for another nap. I was way too excited to sleep. Before my Dad laid down to rest, I asked if I could borrow the tour group roster that he had been provided on the first night. While Dad rested, I picked out "Ms. V Dudoward" upon the list and started working through all the "V names" I could think of—I had to know. We had dinner at the hotel that night and got to bed around 10:30 pm. Sleep was not coming easily with my mind now fully engaged and completely love-struck. Our 6:30 am alarm came way too soon. The mission for August 6th was fairly simple—get ourselves across the Strait of Gibraltar to Tangier, Morocco, on the African continent. As I had never been to Africa, the prospect of adventure was exciting. However, even as my spirits were lifting, our tour group's morale was spiraling downward. The hard schedule and early wakeups were making tempers short and putting health at risk.

We awoke at 6:30 am on the morning of the 6th and had breakfast in our hotel at 7:00 am. After a quick cleanup, we set out on our tour bus at 8:00 am, towards the port at Algeciras. After several hours en route, with a lunch stop in the middle, we finally boarded the ferry at 1:28 pm and the ferry departed an hour later. Our ferry seemed dangerously overcrowded. We were tightly packed, like sardines inside a floating tin can. Unpleasant front-page headlines began circulating through the darker regions of my imagination. While I can't claim to have enjoyed that particular voyage, I did really enjoy getting to see the Rock of Gibraltar as we cruised by. With the boat so crowded, we didn't move around much and I didn't see much of Valerie. I thought about her...a lot. When I did see her, my heart would jump. We finally landed in Tangier, Morocco, and began the painfully slow process of disembarking and clearing through Customs. After the ferry ride, I remember looking out from the bus, watching people behind us come down the ramp. My Dad pointed out some people from our group that were coming off the ship. A few minutes later, Valerie came down the ramp. I doubt my Dad even recognized her as a member of our group. However, as long as he was pointing out people from our group, I thought I'd seize the opportunity to point out Valerie. This was the closest I would ever come to actually tell people that I liked her which was, after all, out of the question. "There's that Canadian lady," I said. This is how I would refer to her when dealing with my family for the rest of the trip even though, a day later, I learned her name by overhearing someone talking about her. Valerie Dudoward!

Rock of Gibraltar as seen from ferry to Morocco (August 6, 1982)

Once we were all on the bus, Maria explained to the group that there had been a hotel mix up and we would have to stay in a cheaper hotel that night. The tourists were all very tired after the hard day and difficult ferry ride. Tempers were running hot. Many of the tourists strongly objected, and I was rather embarrassed by their obnoxious behavior. I was fairly used to mix-ups on our summer trips, and the switch didn't bother me at all. I just wanted a bed to sleep in. We were put up in the Hotel Velazquez, and I thought it was perfectly fine. With my heart spilling over with love, there wasn't much that could bring me down. I took a crash nap a little after 6:00 pm for about an hour, and then joined my family for dinner at 8:00 pm. We were all in bed at 9:30 pm. I began most nights by daydreaming myself to sleep. In some cases, repetitive daydreams were inspired by actual dreams. One of my favorite chivalrous fantasy scenarios (and there were several) was inspired by a warning our tour guide provided regarding motor-cycle purse thieves. In this particular dream, a motorcycle thug drives by and snatches Valerie's purse. Just by a stroke of luck, I happen to be up the street as the villain speeds away with his prize. I make a spectacular jump to knock the thief off his bike and a vicious brawl ensues. The criminal pulls out a knife, and I engage with nothing but my will and chivalrous sense of duty. Well, usually, I got slashed up fairly badly; but as I am being dragged off to the hospital, I hand the bag back to a grateful Valerie. Occasionally, I'd make a spectacular speech before losing consciousness. Sometimes, Valerie would visit me in the hospital and hold my hand as she held vigil. Yes, it was all so easy in my dreams. Real life was not so generous.

The 7th of August began much like most other touring days—an early wakeup followed by breakfast in the hotel. My sister, Jennifer, was very sick and throwing up so Mom stayed with her in the room rather than coming down for breakfast. With Jennifer's health the way it was, my mother remained with her while Dad and I headed out on the city tour of Tangier. While we were out, they'd get transferred to our new hotel (the right one). Tangier was interesting, if a little run down. We spent too much time on the bus as our tour guide talked quickly about the sights we were racing past. We did, occasionally, get out to stretch our legs. As usual, I was constantly aware of Valerie throughout the tour; but I tried very hard not to stare and absolutely avoided direct eye contact. My mind continued to race, grasping for opportunities to engage in conversation. Unfortunately, I was not nearly as smooth in reality as I was within my fanciful dreams. Such is life.

By this time in the tour, Valerie's good-natured persona was gaining her attention; she quickly made friends within the group. The fact that she always seemed to be talking with somebody else made it incredibly challenging for me to even contemplate cutting in and attempting to start a direct dialogue. It's questionable whether or not I would have had the courage to do so, even if the opportunity had presented itself. I was quite jealous of those who did get to spend time with Valerie.

Our Tangier city tour took us to some more "kick-back places" where our local guide clearly had family ties and a vested interest in delivering a large group of paying tourists. While on the trip, a growing number of highly annoying local merchants began following us on their motor scooters. Once our bus stopped, they would quickly unpack their goods and try to sell us the same junk that we had rejected at the last stop—turtle shell guitars, cheap wooden carvings, little brass lamps, and all sorts of assorted trinkets. Later in the afternoon, we stopped at a place offering camel rides. Neither Dad nor I elected to ride. Valerie did. She had a photo taken of her during the ride which, one day, would become incredibly meaningful.

Our tour returned to our new hotel, the Hotel Rif, at 1:20 pm, and we went to check in on the girls. Since they knew my sister was ill, the very nice hotel people gave Mom and Jen an amazing suite at the top of the hotel with a beautiful view out towards the beach and sea. It was spectacular. By late afternoon, Jen was starting to recover. Dad and I went to get a late lunch at the hotel, around 2:15 pm, and ran into several folks from our tour group who all inquired about Jennifer's health. I have to admit that I was a little unhappy with Dad because, each time he was asked, he went into a pre-recorded version of Jen's current status. We bumped into Valerie who also asked about Jen, and I could have just killed Dad when he replayed his very mechanical announcement. Not to Valerie, too! I felt so embarrassed. Lunch was done at half-past three and we returned to the girls' room (because it was ten times more spectacular than ours).

The evening was interesting since we were having dinner at the hotel, and there was a scheduled belly dancing show. I wasn't quite sure what to make of this. Now, even though I was a teen boy,

I wasn't sure I was ready for the experience of having a scantily-clad dancer making her rounds while we dined on Moroccan cuisine. I actually felt somewhat nervous as we sat down to dine. Jen was well enough that she and Mom were able to join us for dinner, at 8:30 pm. A large communal plate of food was placed at the center of the table with no utensils, and tourists at my table looked quizzically at one another, unsure how to attack the strange fare laid out before us. I joked about using my wine glass to scoop out my share for consumption, and I think this helped break the ice at my table—everyone laughed. Funny thing, my sister later remarked to me how she was jealous about how I was so at ease among other people while she was too shy to say anything. If sweet Jenny only knew how horribly shy I felt. I guess life is about perspective. There was no water available for us at dinner so I elected to try a little of the red wine, but not much. Meanwhile, the dancing was starting and my Dad, too, decided to do some icebreaking of his own. I avoided looking at the dancer; but Dad decided to go native and provided a monetary tip for the woman, sliding a bill into her costume, as is customary. After Dad's first move, a number of other equally-impressed men followed suit. Okay, this was a bit embarrassing but you have to give Dad some credit for guts. At age 15, I wasn't giving credit. The show went until 10:20 pm, and I was tired but feeling good. I'm not sure what got into me (perhaps the wine had a greater effect than I anticipated?) but I was fairly spirited at our dinner table and left the restaurant with a smile. On my way up the stairs to the elevator, I saw Valerie dancing with some locals. Yes, I was jealous...but I was also glad she was having fun. I launched into some old Irish folk songs on my way back to the room. As I went to bed that night, I recall hoping that I would still have a little kick left in me, come morning.

August 8th and there was still a little left in the tank. We got up at 6:30 am and then went down to the hotel's dining room for a quick 20-minute continental breakfast. I told my father that I wanted to head upstairs to brush my teeth and get ready to go and then I left him to finish up his coffee. I had waited long enough, hoping that Valerie might join us for breakfast—but she was not to be seen. I made my way to the elevators, just around the corner. As I turned the corner, I got the biggest break of the whole trip. Just coming out of the elevator was Valerie. Some of the kick was still there; and almost out of reflex but with all my heart behind it, I said "good morning." I'm lucky it occurred almost spontaneously or else I probably would have choked, as I usually did when I tried to find words to speak to Valerie. A huge smile broke out on Valerie's face, the most beautiful smile I had ever seen, and she said, "Good morning." Wow! I was completely taken and I literally danced in the elevator all the way up to the fifth floor and then all the way down the corridor to my room, and then some.

We packed up and left our hotel, just after 8:00 am, and I could think of nothing but Valerie as we drove towards the ferry port at Ceuta. The return trip onboard our ferry was a far superior experience when compared to the horrible arrival leg. The ferry was much cleaner and, by comparison, nearly empty. On the journey, Valerie was within eyesight inside the cabin. What to do? In a strange ritual of teenage awkwardness, I pulled out my green rubber ball and innocently bounced it up and down on the floor, only occasionally sneaking a peek at Valerie who, eventually, headed out for some air. Were I not with family, I would have quickly joined her for some sea air upon the deck. In a world of minor victories, breaking the silence barrier earlier in the day was progress enough for me and the moment replayed over and over again in my head.

Our ferry docked at Algeciras at half-past two, and our tour bus picked us up to take us to Torremolinos, on Spain's beautiful Costa del Sol.

Torremolinos was special. It was special in ways I can't fully explain. Besides the natural beauty of the seaside town, the fact that we had a few days of unscheduled rest was very important; and I could feel the empty cup that was my soul slowly filling with fantastic notions of chivalry and knight-errantry. To this point in my life, I don't know that I believed in signs or portents nor can I recall ever having anything resembling a religious experience. Things were changing. As such, I suppose it was no mere coincidence that, at 5:51 pm that afternoon, our bus pulled into our hotel—the Hotel Cervantes. While I had never read *Don Quixote* by Miguel de Cervantes, I was quite familiar with the story of the mad knight who traveled the plains of La Mancha seeking to do good by God and for the sake of his Lady Dulcinea. I found this tale to be particularly compelling—profound, poetic, and beautiful. This was a cause I could identify with—a purpose for life that might, just as easily, be my own. God was speaking to me, and He was laying before me a destiny that was so much grander than the sad and disenfranchised teen existence that had become my prison. More so than ever before in my life, I was ready to listen. Perhaps I could be a knight? Perhaps I could be something more than what I was while not abandoning the inner core of who I was? I began to see a congruency and synergy between the various parts of my personality that had previously seemed completely random and disconnected.

We ate dinner that first night at Pizzeria La Pergola. We enjoyed it so much that we would revisit it several times. After dinner, we returned to our hotel and got to bed somewhat early, except for Dad who stayed up to do some light clothes washing in the bathroom. All of my free time was now completely filled with thoughts and chivalrous fantasies about Valerie. I went to bed feeling very much at peace.

The next morning began an incredible day of complete freedom. There was nothing on our schedule, and the tour group largely disbanded as everyone went off to do their own thing. In fact, my trip log for the day records little else besides breakfast in the hotel followed by lunch and dinner, both at the Pizzeria. For me, however, the day was quite full—daydreams and clever scheming occupied my time. Valerie went to the beach for much of the day and, while my family rested in our hotel rooms, I excused myself and set up a multi-hour stakeout in the hotel lobby. That was a magical time, and I remember it so well. As my eyes scanned the hotel entrance, hoping to see Valerie and create a "chance encounter," my mind drifted away to countless lovely vignettes where I might aid my lady. In some instances, she would enter the hotel, burdened by packages and bags she picked up while shopping; and I would leap up to assist her by carrying her purchases. Sometimes, she'd drop something (even as simple as her kerchief or a scarf) and I would be there to pick it up and hand it to her. In some vignettes, I just said hello and started a meaningful conversation about life. Those dreams were nice. The reality is that I never saw Valerie that afternoon. I returned to our hotel room at a little after 6:00 pm, somewhat disappointed but no worse off for having spent over three hours of quality daydreaming time focused solely on my Lady Valerie.

Sometimes God does grant us moments of relief when we are most in need. I was granted a glimpse of my lady that evening as we walked the pedestrian shopping street not so far from the hotel. My heart leaped at the sight of Valerie not more than 20 yards away. However, before I could do anything, my parents dragged me into one of the stores to show me some stuff. I was desperate to get back out into the street so I stressed that I was not interested in anything. Unfortunately, by the time we finally left the shop, Valerie was gone. I was quite frustrated. We returned to our hotel room and were in bed a little after 10:00 pm.

August 10th. We had a late start to the day, a day designed primarily to take our group on to Grenada. I had no luck spotting Valerie at breakfast. After breakfast, my sister and I went out to the front of the hotel to sit on the steps. Then, much to my great joy, out came Mom walking with and talking to Valerie! I immediately got up and went over to join in. In typical fashion, I choked and barely said anything; but it was still wonderful just to be part of that conversation—to hear Valerie's beautiful soft voice and see her million-dollar smile. She was amazing! Unfortunately, she mentioned that she was going to head to the pharmacy before our bus departed to get some medication because she wasn't feeling very well. I was very sorry to hear this. I tried to think of something I could do for Valerie, but I couldn't come up with any good ideas. There was one thing I could do, though not directly for Valerie. I asked my Mom if we could go back to the shopping street to get something I had seen the night before but decided not to buy at the time. Mom agreed and we raced off to the shops. The bus wasn't scheduled to leave until 10:00 am, so we had time. I believe there must have been some divine inspiration behind this last-minute shopping quest, because the metal knight statue I purchased (or that Mom purchased for me) remains to this day my most prized material possession. The knight embodied my new calling. The fact that I got it in Spain, and when my heart was full of love and concern for my Lady Valerie, has never been lost on me. This statue would later become the centerpiece for a special morning ritual. But for the present time, I carefully packed it away in my carry-on bag. We boarded the bus at 10:00 am and Valerie made it back just in time.

With a pit stop in the middle, we pulled into our hotel in

Granada at 1:25 pm. After signing in at the front desk of the Hotel Luz Granada, we dropped our bags off at our room and headed down for lunch in the hotel at 1:50 pm. After an hour-long lunch and some cleanup, we were back on our bus at 4:00 pm for our tour of Granada. According to the tour brochure, we saw several things that afternoon. The only thing I remember is the beautiful gardens of the Alhambra. While my heart was still focused exclusively on Valerie, my attention shifted towards the lovely pools, fountains, and gardens. I wandered away from my family and the group and did some exploring on my own. I eventually started working my way back towards where our bus was parked, forsaking my usual stunts to time my arrival to match Valerie's (which by now was a regular ritual of mine). Fate is a funny thing. Through no effort of my own, Valerie pulled up beside me, also walking by herself, and we walked together to the bus. It felt so magical to have this brief special time with her. This was also the first time she started a conversation with me. It was hard not to smile as I insisted on Valerie boarding the bus (ladies first) before me. Valerie asked how I did with my camera at the gardens and I told her the truth—that, with the group moving so quickly, I wasn't afforded the time I would have liked to compose and take photos. Valerie agreed. Other tourists were beginning to board the bus so our conversation was rather short-lived as Valerie gained a bus mate and I was rejoined by my parents. The conversation was too short, but it was incredibly meaningful for a love-sick aspiring knight errant.

Alhambra Gardens, Granada, Spain

On our way back to the hotel, our guide stopped at the traditional kickback place to afford the group yet another opportunity
to buy a lot of cheap tourist souvenirs. I was tired and not interested in seeing yet another shop. I stayed on the bus with my
mother and my sister while Dad decided to check out the store.
Fortunately, Valerie remained, too. The bus pulled off to get some
gas, leaving the vast majority of our group at the shop. Mom came
through, yet again, starting up a conversation with Valerie. Even
though I choked, for the most part, I was able to join in the conversation and it was amazing. My Mom told Valerie how I was
keeping a trip log which Valerie thought was really great. My trip
log was really no more than an account of times with little to no
reflection, but I think Valerie was impressed anyway. Valerie had
been keeping a journal, herself. As we pulled into the gas station, I
recall making a rather lame joke about pulling in for a "pit stop." I
immediately felt dumb for even saying it and wished I had been
able to do better. However, dear Valerie was kind enough to laugh

and smile a little, so I didn't feel like a complete zero. Valerie was always wonderful like that. She always did everything in her power to make others feel special, to make us all feel warm inside. Our tour for the day ended at 7:30 pm and after dinner (8:30 pm), we were back in our rooms and in bed at 11:00 pm. I had a lot to think about after the day, so it was a while before I actually fell asleep.

On the 11th, we were up early, at 6:00 am, and scrambled down for a quick continental breakfast in the hotel prior to departing for the morning drive to Cordoba. I was worried about Valerie—her health was not improving, and I desperately wanted to say something to her to wish her health—to do something. Things got worse. Because it was a warm day, many tourists complained that they wanted the air conditioning turned on inside the bus. I typically prefer it warm and, with my jacket always on, the temperature was not a personal issue. It became one, as I saw poor Valerie, without any jacket, sitting towards the front of the bus and shivering. I can't adequately describe how I was being torn up inside. My personal agony was briefly relieved when at least one other member of our group mentioned that Valerie was not well and requested the air get turned off. That reprieve lasted for all of ten to fifteen minutes before another outcry came forth that it was too warm and the air should be turned on. It was. I struggled and struggled, several times nearly getting out of my seat to do what I knew was the right thing. I envisioned a knight boldly marching down the aisle of the bus and then, on bended knee, offering up his prized jacket to keep his lady warm in her time of need. So many times, I nearly did just that. I could feel myself dying inside, but I could not bring myself to overcome my shyness to do the right thing. This failure haunted me terribly for days, and perhaps years afterward. Sometimes, however, God sends us lessons in strange ways. My greatest failure led to a firm vow that I would

never again let my fear dissuade me from doing the right thing—
no matter how awkward or no matter how intimidating that might
be. For the remainder of the tour, I stood perpetually ready to
provide my jacket to Valerie should it rain or if a similar circum-
stance arose. It never did.

We arrived at our hotel in Cordoba, the Hotel Gran Capitan,
shortly after noon, and had lunch before heading out on our city
tour at 3:00 pm. Just prior to the tour, I remember seeing Valerie
outside the hotel—I waved and she gave me a huge smile, said
hello, and waved back. I know these sound like little things now,
but in August of 1982 that might as well have been an embrace and
loving kiss. Our city tour included a visit to the Cathedral, Roman
Bridge, the Emir Fort, and the Jewish Quarter. Throughout the
tour, I desperately tried to maneuver to meet up with Valerie at a
time when she was unaccompanied so that I might inquire about
her health. I failed miserably and, again, my failure weighed
heavily upon my mind. My failure throughout the day, however,
would give way to one of the absolute highlights of the trip. Sometimes destiny works in strange ways. Dinner that night at our hotel
would more than make up for the disappointments of the day.

We went to a group dinner at the hotel at 8:30 pm. Unlike at
many previous dinners, my table was very close to Valerie's, and
with a turn of the head, I had a very good view. Throughout the
tour, I was never blessed with the opportunity to be at Valerie's
table; but I can only imagine that such good fortune might have
presented challenges of its own. As dinner progressed, I found
myself growing less interested in the conversations taking place at
my table. My mind drifted—and then my eyes followed. I found
myself gazing over towards Valerie. Valerie's eyes, likewise, had
drifted away from the dinner conversation at her table. She was
gazing directly at me. Our eyes met. I will never, ever, ever forget
that beautiful moment when our eyes locked onto each other. At

that moment in time, there were only two people in the entire universe, Valerie and me. I was probably a little embarrassed, having been caught red-handed staring at her; and I recall the warm feeling as my face broke out in a confessing blush. As we looked at each other, an incredible smile came upon Valerie's face. I swear that, to this day, I have never seen a smile so beautiful! I felt my face stretch into a huge smile, too. So, there we were, alone in our moment, and it was our moment, looking at each other, both smiling and both aware. My heart completely melted and I was hers. I don't suppose the whole episode lasted more than 10 to 15 seconds, but it was an eternity of bliss. Eventually, we both returned our attention to our respective tables, but my mind was left in a very happy and far distant place—a magical land of dreams.

Dinner ended shortly after 10:00 pm and we returned to our room. I don't think I spoke much for the rest of the night. That special dinner moment played over and over in my head, and I can still see it in my mind's eye. I can still see exactly where Valerie's table was in the dining room in comparison to my own. But, most of all, I can still see that beautiful smile; and this is how I have always remembered Valerie.

The next morning, August 12th, we were up at 6:30 am again for the standard routine of a quick continental breakfast, check out, and a road trip to our next town. The day's drive would be somewhat special as it would take us across the plains of La Mancha—a special journey for a young man only recently allied with the famous knight of Cervantes' imagination.

We departed our hotel at 8:30 am and drove towards Madrid with several stops and a lunch break. I was fully prepared to lend Valerie my jacket and would not fail this time. However, the day was cool enough that there were never any requests to turn on the air conditioning nor any cause for chivalrous deeds. My continued attempts to make contact during breaks also failed miserably. When I write in my diary that I was born on the Plains of La Mancha, it may come across as a figurative reflection; but there has always been a very literal context, as well. Our tour guide specifically noted our journey across the Plains of La Mancha as our bus traveled the landscape made famous by Cervantes. The significance was certainly not lost on me. A number of thoughts and emotions filled my mind and heart. Among these was a growing sadness. I considered that our next stop, Madrid, was to be the final destination on our "Iberian Sunseeker" journey. I could feel a sense of loss building in my heart even though my mind worked hard to remind myself that a final goodbye was still several days away. The things I considered during my daydreaming idle time were also shifting. Rather than running through potential scenarios or ideas for starting up conversations, I began to consider the "what's next" long-term implications for my life. And, as we traversed the magical Plains of La Mancha, a strange notion began to form in my head—I might emulate the legendary knight of La Mancha. I might throw away convention and change my life. Valerie would be my Dulcinea, and I would be her protector and knight. These beautiful yet far-fetched thoughts of an alternative future mingled with my longing and sadness to create a powerful emotional cocktail. My self-identity was formalized, and I felt I finally understood who I was and what I needed to do in life. So, in a manner of speaking, I was truly born on the Plains of La Mancha.

Spanish castle (photo taken from our tour bus)

We arrived at our hotel, the Eurobuilding Hotel in Madrid, shortly after 5:00 pm, had dinner at 8:00 pm, and were in bed at a reasonable 9:45 pm.

On August 13th, we toured Madrid. While in Madrid, we visited the Prado Museum; but otherwise, just raced through the city upon our bus. I was frustrated how quickly we passed by the Cervantes Monument because I really wanted to get a photo; and unfortunately, I was on the wrong side of the bus. On the few stops we did make, I tried to stay near Valerie; and I looked for an opportunity to interact. No moment presented itself, and I felt crushed. Our tour was nearing its end, and I could not overcome my shyness or find the right moment to start up a conversation. I did not want it to seem forced or contrived so I hoped for brief moments that never came. Later in the day, after our tour, I did get to wave to Valerie; she said hello and flashed a lovely smile. That made me feel very good inside. My family had a late lunch at an Italian restaurant that day and, later, dinner at Burger King. I was glad to have a little bit of American food back in my diet; though, in general, the meals during the trip weren't too bad. We got to bed at 10:00 pm, and I went to sleep thinking about our last day of touring. Would I be bold enough to make a move and establish a more meaningful conversation with my dearest lady? Would I somehow be able to eloquently state my feelings or at least express my gratitude for her kind ways and lovely disposition? I did not sleep well.

Monument to Miguel de Cervantes, Madrid, Spain
featuring Don Quixote and Sancho Panza

August 14th was our final day of touring, and we were up at 6:30 am to begin our day's activities which would take us to Toledo. Toledo is famous for many things—the artist El Greco and fine Spanish steel, to name just a few. Unfortunately, for me, it became famous for some horrible diarrhea. I began the morning not feeling well and quickly went downhill. I was no stranger to stomach cramps and diarrhea while traveling, but I was hoping I'd be in my prime for this final day with Valerie. Instead, I sat, doubled over, in the back of the bus, grinding my teeth, sweating profusely, and hoping that I didn't have an accident. I do remember El Greco's home. I didn't even want to move from the bus but I finally did. I hoped I might find a bathroom within El Greco's home. And there was one—but it was a historic bathroom and not for public use. This just seemed to add insult to injury. To make a long and miserable story short, I lost total interest in tracking or communicating with Valerie during this tour. My only focus was to find a restroom, which I eventually did. I don't recall much else about Toledo except that my parents bought me a little sword letter opener with "Toledo" engraved on the blade which I use to this day in various ceremonies. The 14th was an awful failure; and as I went to bed at a quarter 'til ten, I realized any hope of a dashing display of chivalry to gain the notice of my Lady Valerie was totally lost.

Ten days from my 16th birthday, August 15th, 1982, was the gloomiest day I could ever remember. I hardly slept the night before and I was very sad. The dream I was living was about to be torn to pieces before my very eyes and the pieces scattered into the wind. I felt helpless and hopeless.

We woke to our alarm at 6:30 am and went down for our final continental breakfast at 6:50 am. Nineteen minutes later, I was headed back to the room, leaving my father to finish his coffee. I lucked into seeing Valerie at the front desk with another member of our group, so I said good morning to both of them. With minutes dwindling, even such small exchanges had tremendous value to me.

We finished up our packing, boarded our bus for the last time, and were off to the airport. We arrived at Barajas Airport at 8:45 am, after a quick 30-minute drive. I was dying inside, and it was a slow and painful death. I still harbored a dwindling hope of making some final farewell speech; but the when, where, what, and how questions were racing through my brain and the answers were not coming easily. All my senses were on high alert, and I did manage to pick up on a conversation where Valerie mentioned she would not be returning with us to New York. I knew any final meeting would have to take place at the airport.

We got off the bus and went to the airline check-in desk. My parents asked me to watch our suitcases on the long line leading up to check-in. As I stood there between my mother's old white suitcase and my Dad's brown leather suitcase, I saw Valerie walking away towards the far end of the airport and my heart completely sank. I was devastated and felt I had missed my very last chance to say goodbye. My mind was no longer working ratio-nally so I told my parents that I needed to walk around for a little bit, and they conceded. With a very quick step and my heart racing, I headed in the direction I had last seen Valerie. Then, out of the corner of my eye, I saw her sitting down in a row of seats off to the right. I was not mentally prepared to interact just yet so I shortened my stride and continued forward at a much slower pace, trying desperately to work up the courage to engage. Some fifty or so yards later, I slowly began to turn back to where I had just seen Valerie. She was gone! What had I done?! Why hadn't I just gone up and talked to her instead of casually looping back, trying to pretend she wasn't my main objective? These horrible few minutes were, sadly, somewhat representative of most of my experiences upon the trip. My heart propelled me one way, but my silly fear and lack of confidence shackled me. Was I truly that much of a coward that I could not bring myself to say a heartfelt thank you to my Lady Valerie? Self-doubt and darkness swirled about in my teen brain. Now, my goodbye opportunity was truly lost. I wandered about aimlessly for a good 10 minutes or so before finally heading back to rendezvous with my family who were probably still wondering what had gotten into me. When I returned, I could hardly believe my eyes. Not only did I find my Mom but I found her engaged in a one-on-one conversation with Valerie! I quickly rolled in on the conversation. I choked...again. Valerie was telling Mom about how she had sold either some investment or an apartment or something to get the money to go on this trip. My first thought was that this might not have been a wise financial choice; but then, after quickly reflecting, I realized that I would have done the same thing. Money has little value if not for the enrichment it can bring to life. As I anxiously awaited some appropriate moment to inject comments into the conversation, I swayed back and forth and then, even more ridiculously, I walked a circle around Valerie. What was I thinking? I wasn't; I was in love. Valerie assured us that she would see us on the other side of the passport check and would there say goodbye. She also mentioned that, rather than returning to North America, she was taking a flight to Florence, Italy. My heart settled down slightly, realizing I now had a little bit longer to contemplate my final moments with Valerie rather than just a few short seconds. We left Valerie and proceeded through the passport check to the secure side of the airport.

As our boarding time drew nearer and I still did not see Valerie, my heart rate picked up again. Once more, I notified my parents that I was going to take a walk through the terminal. And, once again, at a high speed, I set off in search of Valerie. I checked all the gates for departure information, searching for any aircraft bound for Italy. I was worried that she might have gotten rushed and was unable to drop by our gate to say goodbye, as she had intended. But Valerie was true to her word; and when I returned, she was there to say her goodbyes. I was feeling quite low, thinking about never seeing Valerie again. It was time to board the plane, but I hung back a bit. I wanted just one special moment alone with Valerie, and I got it. There was nothing poetic or eloquent about my words. I just looked Valerie in the eyes, and I believe she could feel the emotion that was bottled up inside me. I said, "Bye."

Valerie looked at me and replied, just as simply, "Goodbye."

Still swept up in her caring gaze, I added, "Good luck," just as I was about to turn back to the gate, with aircraft boarding nearing its completion.

Valerie smiled and said, "Thank you."

The conversation couldn't have been much simpler; and trust me, it has replayed thousands of times in my head over the years. Valerie was the only person on the whole trip that I ever said goodbye to. My honest wish for good luck was all that I could muster up, but it was sincere and from the heart. I always hoped that Valerie was able to pick up on all the small signs and somehow turn my sputtering words and brief comments into eloquent passages of an enamored knight. This was probably too much to hope for; but at 10:50 am at Barajas International Airport on August 15, 1982, as I looked for the last time upon the young Canadian woman I had totally fallen in love with, the farewell scene seemed appropriate enough and did bring some small level of closure for me.

At 11:30 am, TWA Flight 903 took flight and I could not have been more despondent. Some snacks, a meal, and a garbled in-flight movie (*Chariots of Fire*) could not lead my thoughts away from Valerie. I felt like a hole had been torn in my soul. We landed at J.F.K. International Airport in New York City at 12:52 pm, caught an Ollie's Airport Service ride back to Great Neck after processing through Immigration and Customs, and I was back in my own bedroom at 3:15 pm. That was the last entry in my trip log for what will always be my favorite vacation. As I sat in my room, thinking and dreaming, I never could have imagined that August 15, 1982, was not the end of a story but just the closing of the first chapter. Magic and miracles awaited me as did an entire new life and a new way of thinking. Some people spend all their lives searching for God. Sometimes, God finds us.

Chapter Four

THERE'S GOT TO BE MORE

could not get Valerie out of my mind nor did I want to. I was so deeply in love, and that love just kept growing. It was nearly unbearable yet it felt good, too. I knew there had to be more. The story just couldn't end here.

As a personal hobby, I collected weather data every day at 3:00 pm. My brother had taken readings for me while I was in Spain. Interestingly enough, my recorded daily outdoor temperature reading for August 16, 1982, was 82 degrees. The number would forever have special significance for me, and perhaps this small coincidence was the first of many "coincidences" to keep me focused when my mind drifted to less-productive thoughts. Steve Winwood had just released his album *Talking Back to the Night* and his hit single "Valerie" was getting lots of airplay on the radio. *Talking Back to the Night* was released on August 2, 1982—the day I first met Valerie, and the day my life changed. Every time I heard the song, my focus immediately snapped back to Valerie, and I would often sing along. In years to come, the song "Valerie" would make many, many "coincidental" appearances and always when I needed the gentle reminder most. But, I get ahead of myself.

My 16th birthday, ten days after returning from Spain

Several days after our return, I was sitting on an old, green, threadbare, chair in our living room talking with Mom; and we got to conversing about our tour. I don't even recall how we got to the subject; but I'm pretty sure my Mom brought it up when she started talking about Valerie and what a nice, sweet, girl she was. I could only agree! "I wonder what part of Canada she's from," I asked in a desperate attempt to somehow reduce the size of the haystack I would have to search. By this time, I was so passionate that I couldn't imagine my world without Valerie and the crazy notion that we might one day meet again was gaining traction within my thoughts.

"She's from British Columbia," my Mom said.

Holy smokes! I have no idea how Mom gathered that piece of information, but it must have been during one of the numerous conversations she had with Valerie on our tour. This vital information set the stage for my first-ever "Moose Hunt."

Though I did not officially coin the term until a year later, it's appropriate to provide a brief description of what a Moose Hunt is. Moose Hunting was my encrypted way of describing a knightly quest, a pilgrimage, of sorts. These were physical endeavors. They were also spiritual journeys. A Moose Hunt could encompass something as simple as seeking some lead or piece of information related to my lady at the local library. Moose Hunting also encompassed larger endeavors, such as visiting someplace where something special had occurred. I have always maintained a belief that a special kind of magic gets left behind at such places—this magic can help inspire us. The quest, in and of itself, is frequently a spiritual experience that fills my heart and soul with tremendous positive energy. The moose would become my magical questing beast, and images of this magnificent woodland creature would often appear where and when I really needed the reminder. My parents knew better than to ask when my reply to "Where are you going?" was a simple and unelaborated "I'm going Moose Hunting." My mother, especially, the great collector of intelligence data on all her children, quickly learned that it was futile to seek additional clues when my reply involved seeking a moose.

Though not grand on any scale, my first Moose Hunt took me to the Great Neck Public Library where I went directly to the large metal bookcase filled with phone books from the U.S. and Canada. I was really hoping that it would be as simple as finding a large book labeled *British Columbia*, paging through to the Ds, and then finding Valerie's name highlighted in bold text. Unfortunately, our library only had Quebec, Montreal, and Toronto phone books. While a little disappointing, the trip was not a complete loss. Like every Moose Hunt to follow, my thoughts were uniquely pure; and they kept my heart in a good place. I may not have found a thing; but in some small way, I felt a spiritual strength growing within. If you have ever heard the phrase, "It's about the journey, not the destination," then you'll understand the true

value of my Moose Hunting excursions. In days to come, my unde-
veloped early childhood notions of a benevolent "It" protecting
this world, and an invisible friend at my side, began to give way to
some more evolved notions of God and angels. It would be many
years before I would use these terms, but my heart understood.

Failing to make forward progress during my first Moose Hunt,
I knew it was time to enlist the help of my older brother. Oh, how I
wish John could have been on the trip to Spain with us. I'm sure
he and Valerie would have really hit it off. That would have
created an interesting dynamic; but since I never felt I was in
Valerie's league with respect to a relationship, I don't know that I
would have been jealous. My brother has always been the person I
trusted most in this world and, until decades later, was the only
one to even have a slight inkling of how I felt about Valerie.
However, at this early stage, it was critical to not let him know too
much so I left the reasons for my requested trip into New York
rather ambiguous. I wanted to visit the New York City Public
Library and a Rand McNally Map Store. If I could not find a
British Columbia phone book at the New York City Public Library,
then I would have to give up the quest.

At 25, my brother looked rather ragged with his long hair and
unkempt beard. There was not so much as a hint that a comb had
ever made contact with his head. He was my hero! At some earlier
point, presumably during his college experience, John had determined that he was going to live life according to his own rules. He
has always taken the hits for doing so, but that stubborn indepen-
dence perpetually endeared him to me along with an unbreakable
bond between brothers. Ten years older than me, my brother was
both my best friend and, at times, like a second father.

On the 27th of August, John and I hopped on the westbound
train at the Great Neck Train Station and made the thirty-five

minute trip into New York's Penn Station. Both wearing our wind-breakers, we quickly got our bearings and headed directly for the library. The library was a physically beautiful building. The famously imposing stone lions guarded the entrance to this wonderland of literary magnificence. We checked in with the librarian when we arrived; and much to our dismay, were informed that there were over 50 phone directories for British Columbia. Oh, no! We skipped a few of the very small towns but, otherwise, placed our order for all the B.C. phone books available. And then we waited for our number to light up upon the board we fondly referred to as "the bakery number board." When our red number illuminated and the little elevator came up with our books in it, the librarian directed us to a table where we could sit and look through the many assorted volumes. It was immediately clear that this research project would be no small task. With little more said, I asked my brother to take half the pile and write down any name, with corresponding information, for all "Dudowards" that he found. We still joke about this special adventure. For over three hours, we poured through the pages of these phone books while this horrible and erratic modern jazz music played softly in the background. We both had horrible headaches by the time the research was done. The pain was worth it—I walked away with several little note pages with ten to fifteen Dudowards listed. It was a great start, although there was no clear link without a "Valerie Dudoward" appearing in the stacks. The concentrations of Dudowards seemed to be mainly in three areas. This was very helpful and gave me hope.

New York City Public Library

After our time at the library, we visited the Rand McNally Map Store where I purchased a map of British Columbia and one of Canada. I looked for the *Rand McNally Color Guide to Sailing Ships*, but it was not to be found. Many, many years later, it would become my first purchase from a new internet-based bookselling company called Amazon.com.

With maps in hand and my mini-notebook pages carefully guarded, it was time to head for home. This had been a very special journey—the first of several Buddy Moose Hunts where my brother would accompany me, or otherwise assist me, as a willing accomplice on my crazy knightly quests. It's been suggested that I am, perhaps, overly sentimental regarding certain things. I don't view this trait as a weakness. These feelings have driven me to keep many things that others might have discarded. These lovingly-preserved mementos of my journeys still bring me inspiration. The memories come flooding back as I carefully hold these treasures of old.

Since the results of my first two Moose Hunts did not yield conclusive evidence and since I knew it would be several years before I could even hope to stage any trip to British Columbia, I began to worry that I might forget what Valerie looked like. Although her image was still so very clear in my mind and moments from Spain replayed continuously in my head, I knew that time was not on my side. The earliest I could attempt any mission to Canada would be after High School. Would I remember what she looked like? I was kicking myself for not taking a photo of Valerie on the tour. However, I couldn't envision a scenario where I would have. I was too shy to ask to take her photo and too much of a gentleman to try to take one on the sly while she wasn't looking. When my Mom's first set of photos from the trip came back from the photo lab, I desperately hoped that I might find a picture of Valerie in the package. I was very excited as I looked through the photos. Mom and I both had rather cheap 110 cartridge cameras so none of our photos were masterpieces, but amidst the photos of places we visited and things we saw was one that caught my eye. The photo was of the Plaza de España in Seville. In the distance, walking away from the camera, was an unmistakable image of Valerie wearing that pretty purple outfit that I loved so much. I asked Mom if I might have the photo; and without asking any questions, she agreed. While this distant image would never help me to remember what Valerie looked like, it still became a treasured possession. My youthful concerns now seem somewhat silly. They are also somewhat touching. I was so worried that I might, one day, forget which image on the photo was Valerie, that I carefully constructed a plastic overlay which I mounted within a cardboard frame. When the frame was placed over the photo, a penned-in little rectangle identified Valerie's location. I'm pleased to say that I've never had to resort to this navigational aid to find dearest Valerie. I still keep that little frame

as part of my many special memories. Its creation tells a story in
and of itself.

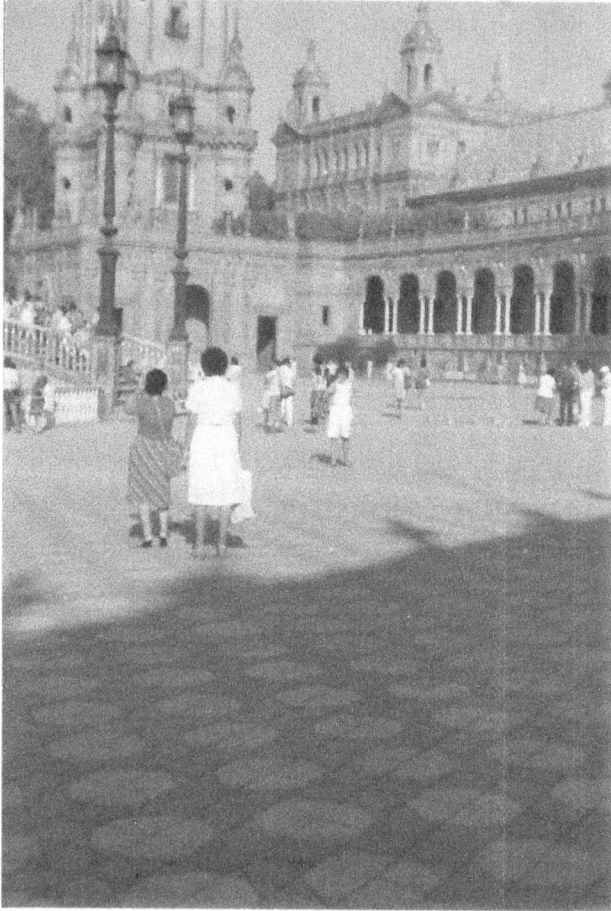

Plaza de España in Sevilla, Spain (August 5, 1982).
Valerie is just right of center, walking away from the
camera.

My days were filled with thought. Upon my green Schwinn
Varsity 10-speed bike, I spent hours and hours riding around
Saddle Rock and dreaming about Valerie. I would circle the
parking lot at the Saddle Rock Park or seek the peaceful paved

playgrounds of Saddle Rock School. Sometimes, as I lazily circled about at Saddle Rock, I could almost see Valerie sitting on the cement steps just outside the gym. And she was watching me. As I rode, I would imagine myself to be a knight of old. My bicycle was my noble charger and I, a brave knight errant. At the upper end of the paved playground, I'd begin to build up my speed, encouraging my mount to run, without fear, towards our foe. As if I were bearing a lance, I'd lower my right arm and lean into the charge. My left arm would raise my shield into position as I prepared for the impact—a clash of warriors upon the field of battle. I would veer off before colliding with the red brick wall of our school. As I passed by where Valerie was sitting, I would remove my baseball cap and salute my lady. Frequently, I would sing songs; but often I would just let my mind race wildly with amazing daydreams of romance and chivalry. It was a special time, and I felt an inner strength growing inside of me. When I wasn't riding, I would walk down to Saddle Rock Park and head down to the water's edge where I would spend vast amounts of time thinking. The frequency of my visits increased greatly in the fall, once all the swimmers and tennis players had abandoned the park and left this holy ground to the dreamers.

Saddle Rock School, back playground

My Schwinn Varsity bicycle by the water at Saddle
Rock Park

Summer was rapidly disappearing, and the prospect of another year of school seemed quite daunting. The previous year had been so sad and so painful; however, Valerie was not going to let me perish.

Up to this point in my life, I had never written anything autobiographical nor had I any notion of keeping either a personal journal or diary. Somehow, I knew that my brief time with Valerie was something very special—it was a story I needed to preserve. Now, it's a well-known fact that most fifteen-year-old boys do not like to write—yet, something inspired me to pull out my typewriter and begin work on what would become a twelve-page typed story simply titled "Valerie." I didn't worry much about grammar or spelling; and I skipped countless details about monuments, landscapes, memorable moments, meals, or anything that was not directly related to the story of my brief time with Valerie and how those moments made me feel. It was truly a labor of love, and I typed passionately with my door closed. My parents must have wondered what had gotten into me. I began writing the day after my trip into the city with my brother; and my work was completed on August 30, 1982. Immediately, I had thoughts of scrapping the whole project and destroying what I had created. This was a high-risk document for me as it revealed a great deal of very personal information: life secrets that I didn't want to fall into the wrong hands. As such, clearly annotated on the title page were the words "TOP SECRET" and "Keep Out!" Even as late as a year later, I considered destroying my creation. I thank God that I did not. To this day, the story brings forth some very powerful emotions when I read it. I read it every August. Often, I will leave an additional comment page, with my thoughts and feelings hand-written, following my annual reading of the "Valerie" story. This simple tale was the story of my life. The moments described defined who I was and who I was becoming. The story opened a new chapter in my life. It may not be a surprise to hear that the very next day, on August 31, 1982, I began Volume I of a diary which I continue to this very day. I learned after writing "Valerie" that there was great value in spending time considering my thoughts and feelings and then writing them down. Much more than a historical record, my diary has become a record of the dreams, life, and travels of this mad knight of La Mancha. My very first diary entry says it all: "My mind still can't stop thinking of Valerie...I must visit her sometime."

With school rapidly approaching, I had much to think about. It would be very hard transitioning back to academics after my recent days of unobstructed daydreaming. As sort of a last Moose Hunt of summer, I visited the Great Neck Library on September 3rd and looked through some college guides. I was hoping to find opportunities for a college education in British Columbia. My institutional requirements had little to do with the curriculum. I was grasping at straws, but I knew I just had to see Valerie again; I was desperate to find some way to move forward with my dream. This was no easy task, given the context of my heavily-restricted teenage world where what was possible often fell short of the desires within my heart. In a time before "computer-based searches" and when phone calls outside of your area code might incur a significant "long-distance charge," journeys such as the one I was envisioning were that much more challenging—especially for a boy on a very private quest.

My dwindling summer days ticked by; each day I would ride my bicycle, think, and stare at the one photo I had with Valerie in it. I still harbored the hope that when my Mom's second roll of film came back from the photo processing lab, there might be another photo with Valerie in it.

The anguish expressed within my early diary volumes was very palpable. I was so in love yet so helpless to do anything about it. On September 3rd, I began a daily count in my diary of "Days Since I Last Saw Valerie." More and more, I was feeling like the lovesick Don Quixote, dreaming forever upon his Dulcinea.

On September 8, 1982, my summer officially ended as I

reported for my first day of 11th grade at John L. Miller Great Neck North Senior High School. I knew that this would be my hardest year of school ever—New York State Regents Exams in nearly every subject and the dreaded SAT exam. There was a lot on the line. My performance during the year would largely determine which colleges I would be eligible to attend.

As I sat in class, I would visualize Valerie sitting at empty desks in the classrooms. She would occasionally smile and wave. I didn't want to forget her, and the best way to remember her was to constantly visualize her during my day.

On September 9th, I was disheartened when the final roll of film from our Spain trip came in and there was no Valerie. On that day, in my diary, I desperately jotted down a physical description of Valerie, as descriptive as a sixteen-year-old could articulate. I was convinced that this description might be my life raft—all I would have to hold on to in the years to come—my only memory of the physical Valerie who I shared time with during a very special summer.

School kept me very busy, and homework filled much of the time that I had happily dedicated to daydreaming during the summer. My only relief from stress was the occasional after school pickup football games that I participated in. Sports were something I greatly missed during the hot and lonely summers.

My nights often ran very late, with time divided between homework and continued thoughts of Valerie. I would often lay awake in bed until well past midnight, when my studies did not already carry me there. The 6:45 am alarm always came too early; and I awoke, inevitably, already exhausted. The days began to blend together yet I found refuge in my newly-created diary. My thoughts were good ones; but I needed to put more measures in place to prevent myself from slipping back into the swamp again, a visualization that would re-emerge repeatedly throughout my life. Within my mind, a new vision for my life began to blossom—a vision of hopping on a motorcycle and riding across the country in search of my lady. In perfect harmony with this vision, the music filling the airways on my radio station seemed to be strangely consistent with the dream. Still, the reality-grounded part of me realized that any plan I formulated would likely have to involve getting a job, raising some funds, and an impossible quest to try to find a woman who, by that time, was likely to have moved, married, changed her name, or perhaps forgotten me altogether. Reality was a painful pill to swallow. I saw no harm in skipping my meds.

Many people search their whole lives to find God and never do. Sometimes, God reaches out and finds us. Sometimes, for no reason we can understand, we are granted mercy from above and given help beyond what we may think we deserve. There are many things I cannot explain. September 18, 1982, is one of those things. I desperately needed help to get life, Valerie and everything sorted out in my brain. I got help.

It was a pleasantly cool Saturday, one which started off with a very unusual and unexplained power failure that lasted for an hour. The skies grew dark in the afternoon, and I felt a calling to head down to the park. As I entered the park and turned to walk towards the fence line separating the tall grass from the choppy sea, the breeze lifted my spirits. It was perfect. The park was deserted, and I perched at the fence and stared out to sea. God spoke to me that day and put a love and understanding in my heart like I had never known. Everything just started to make sense to me. My dark thoughts washed away; and I felt comforted and at peace as I stood there, in my blue windbreaker and baseball cap, soothed by the cool sea breeze. In my diary, I describe it simply in the words of a non-religious sixteen-year-old boy: "I cannot nor will not attempt to explain all the new ideas, etc., that occurred to me today, I will only say how truly lucky I am."

From that day forward, when I would visit the park, I knew I was not alone. The lonely patch of green, where land met sea, became my schoolroom—it was there that God would teach me. I realized that you didn't need to be able to quote a Bible to be a good person. If your faith was true and your heart pure, God might meet you where you stood and teach you, in the simplest terms, what is good and what is bad and what sort of life you were meant to live and how you might honor Him through deeds and beliefs. I would never feel completely alone again, and I thank God and the angels above for that.

There is no easy solution to teen angst, but things began coming together to get me through the hard times. I also found a renewed refuge in music, and the radio often provided songs at the perfectly appropriate time to get me quickly past any dark thoughts. My new anthem became Led Zeppelin's "Ramble On." The song seemed perfectly matched to my vision of riding out to find "the queen of all my dreams."

The long school days and longer school nights continued to wear me down. It was all I could do to hastily scribble down some quick diary thoughts at the end of the day before reclining for some much-needed sleep. I had previously mandated a daily diary entry of at least two pages which, along with other measures I put in place, turned out to be a very insightful decision. Without this self-imposed rule, it would have been too easy to dispense with the therapeutic introspection in favor of an additional thirty minutes of sleep. That would have been a big loss. I was, however, not beyond filling portions of my ruled notebook with various doodles and such in an attempt to compensate for lack of words or lack of time.

Despite the hard schedule, there were bright moments; among

these were some beautiful dreams in my sleep—dreams filled with knights and castles, magic and majesty, and, of course, Valerie. Such dreams helped sustain me through the challenging month of October when I was taken down by a bad case of bronchitis while several other family members fell ill with pneumonia. It was a difficult time.

More and more, I began to vilify school as the guilty party keeping me apart from my lady and slowly crushing my hopes for a happy reunion. School was replacing my happy visions with a dread for the future and a life potentially plagued by poverty—a direct result of my poor academic performance. You should know that I was an "A" student at the time. The incredible pressure put upon all of the "children of Great Neck" was simply mind-numbing and it took its toll on many of us.

It was also during this time that I began to identify not only with knights but so too with the Clint Eastwood character from the Spaghetti Westerns. "The Man with No Name" rides into town, a hero with an edge and a penchant for gunplay. He uses his skills for good but never lets on. He gets beaten down. He returns to wreak unholy vengeance upon the evildoers and sets things right. With no desire for thanks and certainly no need to stick around, he rides off into the sunset. I saw a lot of myself in this character, as well; and during the fall of 1982, these movies were a great inspiration to me. We can fight! We can win!

Throughout the early fall, my studies were pleasantly distracted by daydreams about Valerie; and my nights, often, were filled with real dreams about Valerie. The pages of my diary, meanwhile, filled with random ramblings, frequently about Valerie. But how to honor her? The answer was clear to me. I was to dedicate my life to my lady, and I might honor her best by raising my sword against the foes of goodness. The only place to begin such a boundless battle was by turning, first, within. And so it was. I formulated plans for self-improvement and dedicated all my deeds to my Lady Valerie. First off, there was a daily sword ritual. Standing before my knight statue from Spain, I would carefully raise the metal sword from the knight's grasp and tap it upon my knight's right shoulder, left shoulder, and then helmet. I would then use the same sword to tap upon my right shoulder and left shoulder (as a king or queen might dub a knight) before lifting the sword towards the sky, making my holy vow to fight for the right, and then pulling the sword close to my heart. I didn't do it every day; but when I did, I ensured that I fought hard to keep my thoughts and actions pure throughout the day. This was not always an easy task for a teen boy, but I took my knightly vows very seriously. On those days, when I drew the sword and made my vow, I would put a little card out on my desk saying simply "the sword is drawn" so that there would be no mistake. I wanted to banish all lustful and self-centered thoughts and focus on holy matters. Beyond the sword ritual, I created a television log and limited myself to no more than 10 hours of television a week. I realized at an early age that hours spent in front of the mindless television only drained my passion, strained my eyes, and distracted me from important opportunities for introspection. And on November 7, 1982, I began my first-ever "war game," which I called "Exploring the Enchanted Islands." As part of this war game, I developed a weekly scoring system whereby I could track my path towards self-improvement. Only a positive weekly score would move my piece across a map I created. Forward progress would take me to a variety of mythical islands and locations, and I would not only write my weekly score in a log I kept but also draft a paragraph about my adventures in these fantasy lands. I was learning to fight. This first war game took me all the way to January of 1984.

Knight statue, purchased in Torremolinos, Spain

While all this was going on, I became a regular at Saddle Rock Park. The park would call out to me. Like in the Moody Blues song, "Tuesday Afternoon," I could feel something calling to me; I just had to head outside and down to the water's edge. As I looked out upon the water, with the blissful autumn breeze blowing in my face, I would drift off into another world. Songs I had never heard before would fill my head, and I would sing them aloud. Their rhyming verse was always quite astonishing and pleasing to me, and the lyrics always seemed to carry an important lesson. I was being taught. I became convinced that divine spirits were putting these words in my mouth; and I felt so very spiritually strong, as I stood there, singing in the vacant park. There were several songs that would start the same but quickly wander off upon a fantastic lyrical journey. One such song was the knight song. To this day, when I feel a certain magic in the air, and I know I am alone with divine Friends as my only audience, I will be inspired to sing: "When day turns to night and there seems little light, there's a man who will stand, who will fight, for the right of that wonderful, magnificent, triumphal and beneficent knight..." I never know what follows. There were other songs but the knight song was the most frequently recurring and would occasionally go on for fifteen minutes or longer—each time with new and meaningful lyrics. Because these songs were first given to me in the Autumn of 1982, I still refer to them as "Autumn Song." I believe they are one of the ways God passes messages and lessons to me.

Time moved on but my heart never did. My diary entries continued to reflect a longing for she who had stolen my heart, and countless lovingly-penned entries extolled the virtues of my dearest lady. Clearly, there was some pain and sadness but this passion gave me strength and focus. I truly could "love pure and chaste from afar," as the lyrics of "The Impossible Dream" describe. I completed reading a biography of Miguel de Cervantes that fall and grew increasingly devoted to the calling of knight-errantry. While my Dad would clearly not take kindly to me reading holy books, I knew there would be no concern with me immersing myself with tales of chivalry and such. And so, like Don Quixote, I would absorb any television show, magazine article, or book having to do with knights and the age of chivalry.

On November 23rd, I saw a television "travel log" about Vancouver and became convinced that if I were to ever find

Valerie, then this is where I must start. The timing of the show, like other events before, did not seem coincidental to me. The show aired on the 100th day since the last day I had seen Valerie. There was no doubt in my mind that Valerie was still with me and that she was helping me. I only wanted to thank her and do anything in my power to return her favors.

As winter approached, my days remained filled with Valerie daydreams. Valerie dreams by night were far less frequent occurrences and, consequently, gained my undivided attention and analysis when I was fortunate enough to wake and remember them. Many seemed to carry special meaning. I documented one very memorable dream from December 6th—it struck me as being incredibly real. In the dream, I was sitting on the soft grass of Saddle Rock Park by the water's edge. Valerie passed by, walking with someone else. As you may recall, this inability to find time alone with Valerie was a source of frustration for me during our trip. She was wearing a tennis dress. I waved. She waved back and continued on. I felt an incredible and desperate need to follow her, but she was already walking out of sight. I hurried home and got my bicycle and rode, and rode, and rode until darkness fell, pedaling frantically. I continued through the pitch dark of night, but I could not find her. When I awoke, I felt so very sad. This was one of several Valerie dreams that went well beyond my normal V-dreams in that the entire experience seemed incredibly realistic and life-like. Perhaps they were real? I will never know, but the rational part of me doubts this possibility. Four days later, I would have another realistic Valerie dream. I took them as signs, though I don't know that I deciphered the messages beyond that. I did not want to "put words in God's mouth," so to speak; but I could not help but feel that He was trying to tell me something; God or his angels. I was not understanding. Then again, perhaps I was.

The holidays came and went and, before you knew it, 1982 was history. The new year came with new doubts, but it also came with new Friends. There was also a renewed commitment to the lady who started it all.

Chapter Five

ANOTHER WOMAN!

*A*s I journeyed down my solitary and very unconventional path, I looked for signs to guide me. Having not read from the Bible, nor been instructed in any faith, I had to rely on the hope that God would put the right things in my heart and guide me through signs and portents. Often, things did not make sense to me; but where I felt some divine inspiration, I followed nonetheless. On the evening of January 8, 1983, my family and I were watching *Fantasy Island* on television and the special guest star was Dorothy Hamill. I took note.

Back in 1976, you see, I had the most tremendous crush on Dorothy. She was the lovely and shy nineteen-year-old who won the Olympic Figure Skating gold medal in Innsbruck, Austria. She also won America's heart. I was only nine at the time, but I was clearly distracted by Miss Hamill's beauty and charm. At school, in my fourth-grade classroom, I felt an irresistible pull towards "the book nook" in the back corner of our classroom. A recent addition to the collection was the February 23, 1976 edition of *Sports Illustrated*. Within the magazine was a full-page color photo of

Dorothy, smiling as she stood atop the victory podium. In between actual school work, I would regularly sneak back to gaze upon the photo. At home, my younger sister was the recipient of any Dorothy Hamill material that made its way into magazines or newspaper articles. I was so enamored with the photo from the *Sports Illustrated* issue that I asked my brother if he could get me a copy of the magazine. He walked into town and visited our regular stationery store. Unfortunately, when he got there, he discovered that the new week's edition of *Sports Illustrated* was already out on the newsstands. Being the awesome brother he was, he asked the salesperson if they still had any of the previous week's edition around. They went in back and physically cut open a box that was filled with old magazines to be shipped out. After a bit of digging, the manager was able to find a remaining copy of the magazine. My brother bought it and began his walk back home. John never asked for any reimbursement. I think he understood the value, and his compensation was something that money couldn't buy. I used to look at that magazine every night before bed, and I'd drift off to sleep with a peaceful and happy heart.

Seeing Dorothy on *Fantasy Island* in 1983 sparked something deep inside of me. I felt inspired. Could I have two ladies? Was this being unfaithful to my Lady Valerie? There were lots of questions to answer. In time, the answers would come. The answer to the first question was "yes," I could look to two ladies for inspiration without being, somehow, unfaithful. I became vigilant for signs related to either. On January 10th, I committed myself to both. The duel-commitment was not something I took lightly; and I was very concerned that I never back away, in any way, from my love and commitment to Valerie.

The Moose was on the loose and, as might be expected, I found it easier to conduct Moose Hunting research adventures in search of information about Dorothy. While not as ever-present as she was in the mid-70s, there was still a sizable volume of data to be mined regarding a U.S. National, Olympic, and World figure-skating champion and American celebrity. Beyond reading up about Canada, there were far fewer options to draw me closer to my lovely friend from the North. I made do with books about knights, castles, and chivalry. In the course of my activities, I made frequent trips to the library and spent time with the *Reader's Guide to Periodical Literature*. In my search for articles about Dorothy, I discovered she had married in 1982. Ah, two ladies, and both an impossible distance away. I was not deterred. My inspiration came not from what they might offer me but, instead, from who they were as people. Both inspired me to complete my first perfect week of battle in my war game (January 15, 1983). It was possible! That day, I read an article on Dorothy that I had copied from a magazine. I also re-read my "Valerie" story. I would honor both my ladies. My diary entry for the day closed simply with "Happy Anniversary, Dorothy" and "Thank you, dear Valerie."

On January 25, 1983, 163 days since the last time I saw Valerie, I closed out Volume I of my diary. It could very well have been the only volume. Some inexplicable force bade me to continue. For my first diary volume, I had required myself to write two full pages per day. This was a good plan to get me started. I relaxed the requirement for Volume II. I still insisted upon a daily entry, but there would be no need to fill physical voids with random scrib-bling or generously spaced words. Future volumes would remove the daily requirement, all together. The one thing I notice most when I look back upon my first diary volume is that, beyond just the words, a surprising theme was developing—I was starting to like myself again. This may seem like a minor point; but for me, it represented an incredibly important shift in my psyche.

As the days rolled by, school trials created a challenging balancing act—hopes and dreams on one side and the stark reality of a performance-based road to "success" on the other. My diary entries still focused primarily on Valerie, although there were times when they strayed, without guilt, to Dorothy Hamill. Dorothy was something I could explain away to my family, but Valerie was still deeply personal. As I battled exhaustion and self-doubt, my ladies continued to inspire me. Beyond the walls guarding my chivalrous dreams, high school baseball was one of the few high points in life. Unfortunately, the '83 season was my least successful. Successful or not, I still loved playing; and I appreciated the comradery that came with being part of a team.

Another highlight from the spring of '83 was my completion of the SAT exam, on May 7th. Like some epic beast from mythology, for years it loomed in the darkness of its bone-filled cave. All of us knew we would have to face it eventually. Each day drew us ever closer to the confrontation, and there seemed that no volume of training or preparation was likely to ready us for the fateful encounter. As such, free time was never really free. I always felt that I should be studying. As if my own sense of study-guilt was not vicious enough, my mother would constantly remind me that I should be working on my vocabulary words or spending more time with my SAT preparation workbooks. I never did "finish" studying. Does anyone? Perhaps my only consolation from this miserable experience is that I am now fairly articulate when it comes to words beginning with the letters A through I. That's as far as I got.

With the SATs out of the way, it didn't take long to get back in the fighting spirit. However, I wasn't out of the woods yet. My most challenging barrage of New York State Regents Exams lay ahead, and just a month away. As with all the trials we face, these, too, would eventually pass. I had been moderately successful with the SATs. My New York State Regents results were an academic tour de force. I felt very satisfied. The 1982-1983 academic year had been a brutal experience. And then it was over. On June 23, 1983, this most horrible year of school finally came to an end. I was victorious, but only with the help of my Friends. The war references increased in my writings; and more and more, I began to view life as a battle—a struggle of good against evil. An earthlier version of this struggle would play out before me that summer, as my family took a 23-day tour of the Soviet Union.

The trip to Russia, which took us to numerous cities, reaffirmed every opinion I had about the perils of life behind "the Iron Curtain." I returned with a renewed appreciation of the true blessings of living in a free country like the United States. Though I was already interested in the United States Air Force before going on this trip, my passion increased ten-fold after completing the tour. A future in the U.S. Air Force seemed like a fitting occupation for an aspiring knight, and the noble thought of fighting to preserve our American freedoms and liberty was something that fit perfectly with my desire to do something larger than myself. To sacrifice all in the name of a just and good cause—I could do that.

From a daily life standpoint, the remainder of the summer of '83 could probably be categorized as boring. Great Neck was a ghost town during the summer, and I spent my days riding my bicycle around the area. All of my friends were out of town for the break. From a spiritual standpoint, I was ramping up to fight my first official "battle."

Chapter Six

THE WAR YEARS

*A*ugust 2, 1983, was the first anniversary of the day I met Valerie, a day that marked a momentous change in my life. To commemorate the special day, I elected to embark upon yet another "self-improvement" endeavor. In the parlance of my developing life view, I planned to initiate my very first "battle," in an effort to further cleanse and purify my soul on my ill-defined journey towards some form of Heaven-granted knighthood. My August 2, 1983 diary entry describes my plan:

> *Well, it's been 12 months, one whole year, since the day I first met Valerie and started up the battle. Today is the first anniversary. It is on this day that I now propose to enter into the grandest battle I have yet waged in my war game, a game in which I must truly fight. In this confrontation, the Anniversary Battle, I will do something I've not dared to do before. I <u>will</u>, by my honor, (I am sure I will later regret this but in the end be oh so proud of my fight) win a consecutive 30 days of battle to demolish the old record of 25 which was set after the greatest struggle and best roll I was ever on. I must consider it an act*

of dishonor if I in any way attempt to back out of my proposal (with
less than 30 days of victorious battle). I shall live in shame if I try to
destroy this page or any other records of my commitment. In honor of
Valerie and my decision to go to war, I <u>shall</u> return victorious. Mark
my words—30 days. I will no longer speak of strength and pride if I do
not pull out this one, great, Anniversary Battle, ever again. My words
are harsh and strong, as are the battle terms, but I've got to do it, no
backing out. I now, officially, declare war and so the battle begins,
Charge!

And thus, I began my very first battle, "The Great Anniversary
Battle." I would draw my sword each morning and make a solemn
pledge to abide by the strict rules of conduct I had established for
myself. Always, my focus would be on spiritual matters as I sought
to drive from my mind any and all thoughts I deemed not in line
with my honorable intent. I would honor Valerie, but I would also
honor God and my "Friends," friends who I felt were looking out
for me from Heaven. Angels? Perhaps. For me, they were simply
"Friends"—true friends. I felt immense gratitude for having been
given a second chance in life, and I was adamant not to betray
their trust by falling back into my old ways after they had given me
support and inspiration beyond what I felt I deserved. It was as
simple as that. My battle was my way of saying "thank you," and
this very first battle was an amazingly powerful and inspirational
experience.

I also began a yearly tradition of re-reading my Valerie story
every August so that I would never forget. It's somewhat amusing
that the first annual comments (August 7, 1983) I added to the story
are a bit derogatory. I call my own story "confused and poorly written." In future years, I would self-critique my own ridiculous
critique. The story remains a beautiful inspiration. While I don't
add notes every year, the numerous remarks I have made form a

wonderful commentary on the impact of the story, and the events of 1982, through various phases of my life.

With some driving lessons and football games mixed in, I successfully fought my way through August 31st and concluded my first-ever battle. This was, in my world, a monumental achievement. I felt very proud. More so, I felt very thankful. I could not have done it alone.

From a historical perspective, the time from when I first met Valerie until the time I left for college was a period I designated "The War Years" because the days were filled with fighting internal battles to better myself, ensuring I didn't stray from the path. I felt I had a destiny to fulfill. I knew the only way to achieve my purpose was to keep my heart true and my soul pure. The fight was on! The next form of battle rapidly shaped up—it was a "drive for as long as you can" fight that differed from a pre-specified holy vow with clear time limits. On September 4th, with little diary fanfare, I began "The Great Autumn Offensive" which shattered all previous battle records, doubling even my best effort. I was on my way and getting stronger with each effort.

Battles were often accompanied by the soundtrack of my life— inspirational music which would drift through the airways and lovingly trace the wires to the less than professional quality speaker of my flip clock radio. These songs would make their glorious entrance at just the right moment in time and make an impact upon my psyche. My Friends (with the capital "F") reached out to me in the dream world, too. I considered myself fortunate, basking in an impressive array of dreams including some very memorable tales of chivalry. One dream stands out especially—it was a recurring dream and one that seemed to carry an important message. I don't recall the first time I had it, nor the last. What's important is that I have not forgotten the imagery nor the message. I can still see the scene quite vividly in my mind—the dream has saved me more than once. The story begins upon a vast grassy plain. In the distance, a large castle dominates a hilltop. In the foreground, there is a beautiful woman who beckons me closer. Her hair is dark and wild, like some beautiful gypsy. Her eyes are enticing and very provocative. The mysterious woman is dressed in courtly garb. She is extremely attractive. Appareled in full armor, and riding upon my charger, I slowly advance towards the woman. As I draw nearer, I notice how sexually appealing she is. She is beautiful and her low-cut bodice reveals a little too much cleavage. I feel myself slowly falling under her spell. The woman's sexuality, her dark and welcoming eyes, and her mannerisms draw me ever closer. Like a sailor, entranced by the siren song of a mermaid, I find myself unable to resist the temptation. Nearly hypnotized, I ride forward. Then, out of the corner of my eye, I see another woman. This woman is, likewise, dressed in medieval court attire; but her purple dress is much more modest than the garments worn by the temptress before me. It is Valerie! My Lady Valerie! She does not motion to me or otherwise attempt to draw my attention. Lady Valerie gazes upon her knight with a caring eye. She need do no more. Despite the allure of the temptress, I turn my horse and ride towards Valerie. The spell is broken. Enraged, the temptress transforms into a horrifying demonic monster and charges towards me to finish her lethal work. I quickly reel my horse about, couch my lance, and charge the beast at great speed. After a terrible crash, a vicious battle ensues. Though bloodied and physically exhausted, I finally strike the death blow—the battle is over. I return to the pure and welcoming arms of my Lady Valerie. We rejoice in each other's company. And this is where my dream always ended. The several times I experienced this dream were amazing spiritual experiences. I felt God was sending me a clear message. The message was to stay away from sex and foul temptresses and focus your love on innocence and purity. It is a message I've never forgotten and advice I live by. It is not my place to pass judgment upon others and the choices they make. And rarely will I do so. However, I know well the road I am meant to journey, and I'll fight any and all temptations that attempt to drive me from my path.

Autumn, my favorite season! Fall of 1983 brought lots of great pick-up football games and positive life events that helped to keep my morale up. My parents never knew I was playing tackle foot-ball with my friends, but our pickup games were a true highlight of the school year for me. I did my best to hide torn jeans, bloodied knees, the occasional limps, and, in one instance, a jacket that was literally torn in half down the backside. I also learned to drive in the autumn of 1983. While I didn't own my own car until many years later, having a driver's license seemed to open up a whole new set of possibilities for future questing. This was a crit-ical skill I knew I would need if I were ever to stand a chance at realizing my dream to find Valerie. For friends—their wheels meant movies, concerts, dinners, and dating. My focus was elsewhere.

Autumn soon gave way to winter and the new year. With SATs, Achievement Tests, and additional milestones falling before me, I found myself rapidly steaming towards the end of my high school "career." During my final year, there was an interesting addition to my portfolio of school activities. During gym class, my physical education teacher saw how fast I was during a football game. He happened to also be the coach for the Varsity Swim Team. I believe he translated speed on the field with velocity through liquid mediums. Perhaps it was that I was tall and had long arms? Whatever the case, he asked if I would consider trying out for the Varsity Swimming Team. This was very unexpected. I also found it somewhat humorous because I hadn't done any swimming since my elementary school days, and I was not completely confident that I could even stay afloat. I expressed my concerns, but Coach Hugo felt he could work with me. Considering that I would need to be proficient in the water to complete the graduation requirements at the U.S. Air Force Academy, I thought this might be a worthwhile endeavor. So, I showed up for practice. As I imagined, I was barely able to keep my head above water. But, true to his promise, Coach Hugo and his assistant coach worked with me and another "newbie" to help us along our counter evolutionary journey from land back to the sea. I doubt I contributed very many points over the course of the season, but I did enjoy being part of the team and competing against other schools. The practices were very grueling. I worked hard to improve my swimming ability. I knew my willpower would be tested, were I to be accepted at USAFA. Hopping into a cold pool and swimming myself to the point of exhaustion was a good first step along the road to overcoming physical pain and mental barriers. In a way I did not fully appreciate at the time, my experiences with the swim team would later pay great dividends. I can thank Peter Hugo for giving me that opportunity—one that I would not have sought on my own.

In February, I began what I would consider, for many years, my greatest battle. I determined it was time to dedicate one to Dorothy and so, on February 1, 1984, I began "The Great Ice War." My battle would get a big boost with the opening of the 1984 Winter Olympics, on February 8th. This was a magical time, and I could feel many positive forces coming together. Academic stress and physical exhaustion could not keep me down. Our winter break afforded me a great opportunity to recover from the sickness that had been plaguing me. My sister, Jennifer, and my Mom headed off on their trip to Austria on February 11th, leaving "the boys" home to watch the Olympics and goof off. With the Olympics in the air, Dorothy was all over the television—interviews, a professional's figure skating competition, soft drink commercials, etc. On February 10th, I remark:

I am rolling, and better than ever...I'm just sorry I won't be able to go see Dorothy in Ice Capades, but I did try. Until I'm on my own in the world, I won't be able to always get things like that, things which I really want.

On the night of the 11th, my fighting spirit kicked in. Rather than grimly resigning myself to accept a reality that was less than my dream, I decided to take the offensive. Good intentions were not good enough—not for a dreamer! Ice Capades had one remaining day at Madison Square Garden. There was still hope— still a chance to cross that bridge into my world of magic and dreams. With no tickets in hand, and unable to get through by phone to the ticket counter, I enlisted the help of my brother. John had saved the day before. Memories of his exploits during the *Sports Illustrated* quest came flashing back. Although Mom was on the road, I still had doubts that my father would be excited about me traveling into Manhattan alone, even though I was seventeen. My brother was ready for another Buddy-Adventure. And thus, our quest began. We made our way to the Great Neck Train Station and, again, boarded the familiar westbound train into the City. We still had no idea if any seats would even be available. Fortune was to smile upon us that warm winter's day. Not only were seats available, but we managed to secure some very good seats. I was very excited! The show was quite magical, and I was entranced through Dorothy's three performances. While the overwhelming quantity of children in the audience may have shifted the audible fan appreciation volume in favor of the Smurfs, I did my best to equalize the applause register. The birds were singing, quite literally, as we returned from Manhattan. This adventure remains one of the greatest highlights of the "War Years." It's an adventure my brother and I often reminisce about. Setting out empty-handed, with only faith to drive us, we turned the day into a special and magical one. Perhaps it's more appropriate to appreciate that this special and magical day was given to us—it was a gift. Such moments of faith-driven euphoria must surely be Heaven-sent. I still believe it was. The advertisement that caught my eye and my ticket stub are still carefully preserved in the pages of my diary.

A few days later, I was Moose Hunting yet again. This time, my quest was to acquire a copy of Dorothy's new autobiography. I hopped in the car with my Dad and brother, as we went to drop John off at the train station to head back into Manhattan. My plan was to depart from the train station and walk back home after visiting the book store. I only had six dollars in my pocket; and my brother, suspecting my intent, gave me some more cash before departing. It's a good thing he did. I needed it. Shortly after being dropped off in the middle of town, the severe stomach cramps set in. This was not unusual for me. I've always had a history of gastrointestinal tract challenges which made life a little more "interesting." My first thought was: "How in the world am I going to make it home without having an accident?" I've grown to accept this physical nemesis as not only a part of life but also a frequent companion upon my quests and adventures. Perhaps my mind works in odd ways, but the pain and suffering always tended to add a certain epic quality to my quests. If you really want something, you've got to earn it. If you really believe in something, you have to be willing to suffer some for the sake of your cause. Good works without sacrifice have less spiritual value. So, there I was, alone and suffering with two choices. I could head directly for home and hope that I could make it before disaster struck or I could push on with my quest and hope that I could complete the trial before a horrible accident ruined my morning. I struggled into the largest bookstore in town and began my search. In great pain and discomfort, I searched the shelves to no avail. There was no public restroom in the store. I grew desperate. I was about to head for a public phone to call my Dad to retrieve me, but something inside inspired me to keep pushing on. I actually did start to head for home but then recalled that there was one more book store in town, a much smaller store called The Little Professor. The Little Professor was less than a half-mile away. A half-mile, in my current condition, was no small distance. I knew it was my last chance. I quickened my pace, gritted my teeth, and tightened up my stomach muscles. My perseverance was rewarded. Shortly after entering the establishment, my eye caught sight of the unmistakable beautiful face of Miss Hamill smiling back at me from the cover of her book. I was overjoyed and grabbed the only copy of *Dorothy Hamill: On and Off the Ice* that the store had. As mentioned, I needed the extra money my brother had given me to make the purchase. With book in hand, I plotted a direct course for home and picked up the pace. My health seemed to improve as I traveled, and I began to sing and hum songs. One final bit of drama capped this adventure. With only about 1/3 to 1/4 mile remaining, I realized I had promised I would record a television show for my sister; and I was only three minutes away from breaking that promise. With my remaining energy, I sprinted the all uphill remaining quarter mile of my journey and made it just in time to get the videotape in and hit the record button! What an adventure! If you want something, you've got to earn it.

While Dorothy dreams carried me through February and to a victorious completion of the incredible "Great Ice War," it is important to note that my heart never left my Lady Valerie. In days to come, there would be others who would inspire me; and often, God would put them in my dreams and send signs to me in my waking hours. I would be a fool to shun such divine inspiration and so I never did. While writing this story, I considered keeping only to those segments directly related to Valerie. I realized this would leave voids that would remove some very beautiful events and even a few amazing miracles. The story is not complete without these and so I continue.

In February, I began a new War Game. "The Great Ice War" ended and so, too, the Olympics and my winter vacation. It had been a magical and spiritually rewarding time. My focus shifted towards my final season of high school baseball, even as I was finishing out my high school varsity swimming experience. My immediate and most concerning obstacle, the Air Force Academy Candidate Fitness Test, was scheduled for February 26th. On that day, I awoke feeling sicker than a dog...a really miserably sick dog! My father drove me into Brooklyn, to Fort Hamilton, to take the Fitness Test. I was curled over, fighting to hold in my diarrhea, along the way. We arrived at the pre-appointed time. I was feeling defeated before I had even changed into gym clothes. It did not help that the room was filled with guys twice my size, all with impressive Letter Jackets on. I felt like I was a bit out of my class. Were these the brutes who filled the ranks of our military services? With my focus still on my stomach condition, I didn't spend too much time considering the competition. After a brief introductory presentation, all the test takers were released to the locker rooms to change. I made a direct line for the toilet. After clearing my system, I began to steel myself for the coming challenge. There's always been a part of me that was able to reach down deep for something a little extra. I started reaching. Beyond any adrenaline boost that I can possibly claim credit for, I am quite convinced that the angels above were looking out for me, too. As I began the test, I quickly realized that I was NOT out of my class. I was scoring higher on the various components than all those "giants." I DESERVED TO BE THERE! I deserved to be there, and I was going to fight to follow my dream. It was an amazing day, and I found strength I never knew I had. I performed better than I had during any practice session. When the test was done, I had convincingly passed all of the components and was deemed well-qualified, physically, for an Academy appointment. It was a tremendous victory. I knew where the credit belonged. I was grateful and in a peaceful state of mind for the long drive back to Great Neck.

College was looming in the distance. I had been accepted at a number of universities but was still awaiting a reply from my first choice—the United States Air Force Academy. Regardless of which school I attended, I knew my life would soon be dramatically changing. It was a daunting thought. With the coming of March, I knew there were plenty of late nights of high school studies left and a season of baseball games to be played...but the ticking of the clock was growing ever-louder.

On April 18, 1984, after coming home from baseball practice, my parents directed me towards a letter, placed prominently upon my desk. The letter was from the office of Senator Daniel Patrick Moynihan. Earlier in the year, I had interviewed for and received his nomination for an appointment to the Air Force Academy. I opened the envelope with care. Finally, the news I had been hoping for! The letter was a personal congratulations from the Senator on my acceptance at the United States Air Force Academy! I was absolutely overjoyed. My life was about to make another significant maneuver—things would never be the same.

In the dwindling months of my civilian life, there remained a few more battles, a few more tests, and a whole lot of fitness activity to help me prepare for the Academy. I also spent a vast amount of time reminiscing about the past. Many of these sentimental journeys took me to special places from my childhood. It's interesting that I was so nostalgic at such a young age. I think I was very aware that my life was on the verge of changing very dramatically. I knew I would have to contend with an array of challenges that none of my high school classmates would ever have to deal with...nor be likely to comprehend. I was now accelerating forward on an irreversible path.

My last day of class was on June 14th. On June 21st, my classmates and I graduated from John L. Miller Great Neck North Senior High School. It was the end of my childhood. "The War Years" officially ended on July 5, 1984, and I began my new life on July 6, 1984—the day I began Basic Cadet Training at the U.S. Air Force Academy.

Chapter Seven

THE ACADEMY

Basic Cadet Training (BCT) photograph, July, 1984

The Air Force Academy and I were never a perfect fit. However, we got along where and when it mattered most. My crazy dream to be a "knight of the skies" propelled me through years of great hardship. My inspiration to carry on was always my faith, my ladies, my dreams, and my quest. I could easily dedicate an entire novel to my experiences as an Air Force cadet, but these stories would lead us astray from the story I truly wish to tell. So, I shall purposefully race through trials and tribulations, triumphs and failures, and countless stories, all worth sharing, so that I might remain on topic. I will say that my first year was a living Hell. Several individuals, for one reason or another, decided early on that I did not live up to their expectations. It may have been because I was a New Yorker. It may have been because I did not go to church. It may have been because they sensed a defiant individualism within me that refused to be broken or toyed with. Regardless, I quickly found myself on the receiving end of a terrible slander campaign. My footing was not so solid as to be able to quickly turn the tide of this negativism. It would take time. My progress would be measured by one upperclassman at a time. By this, I mean that I had to convince each individual above me (sophomores, juniors, and seniors within my squadron) that I not only cared about the Academy and my future in the military but also that my performance was at least on par with my classmates and not, contrary to the slander campaign messaging propagated by a few jerks, sub-standard. I was yelled at constantly. I was rarely allowed to eat, as I was perpetually assigned to "the training table" where lunches were spent getting yelled at and not eating. When I should have been studying, my grades falling like a rock, I was out reciting Air Force quotes, meal menus, every bit of Air Force trivia imaginable, and I was being tasked to write reports on various aircraft and other military subjects. I had to spend more time on perfecting my uniform and military appearance because I was judged much more harshly than any of my classmates. With all the extra work and the mental distress, I came very near to failing out of the Academy that first year. Somehow, I survived. Amidst this on-going academic battle, I continued to press my limits to achieve military excellence. One by one, my true performance began to win over upperclassmen; and a growing number of these cadets began to understand the wrongs that had been done to me. By April, things had improved (albeit not academically) and the only upperclassmen who seemed reluctant to acknowledge my accomplishments were the one or two individuals behind the dark plot to eliminate me. Even they backed off and turned their hazing imaginations towards other endeavors. On May 23, 1985, the Class of 1988 was "recognized," after a less than enjoyable "Hell Week." Recognition is a long-standing tradition at the Academy whereby the under-classmen ("4 Degrees" or "4th Classmen") gain status within the wing and are no longer treated as second class citizens. Needless to say, this was a time of great joy for me and my classmates. I felt very proud when a number of the upperclassmen in my squadron noted my "toughness" at sticking it out throughout all the personal challenges that they knew I was subjected to. I never forgot.

The following years were primarily academic struggles—I had figured out the rest of the service academy formula for success. For me, working my way through advanced engineering courses within the limited time constraints of the Cadet Duty Day was tantamount to navigating an academic minefield. Thankfully, I no longer faced any issues with people or "the establishment." My first year, unfortunately, had been more about defiance and not letting the Academy beat me. My remaining three years were more focused on what the Academy was truly about—growing into a professional officer and leader. Through it all, however, I never completely felt like I belonged. I overlooked these sentiments and kept my focus on the mission. I was tracking towards a goal and my level of comfort simply didn't matter. My job has never defined me. The spirit within my breast and the passion within my heart are what make me who I am. I was compatible with the Air Force, and the Air Force never forced me to become something I was not. We got along where it mattered most.

I do believe that someone was watching out for me during these challenging years of my life. My faith was solid, but the occasional "coincidences" or small miracles were welcome gifts and helped to both carry me through the times of doubt and also springboard me into a euphoric state of exhilaration during times of strength and stability. My Moose Hunts continued and grew in scope during my time at the Academy. God was kind enough to leave me signs to help guide me on my spiritual journey.

June 9, 1985. My Academy sponsors were a husband and wife pair of Air Force Master Sergeants. On this particular day, Master Sergeant Burns took me out to the Academy archery range with one of his buddies. They were both excellent archers and frequently bow hunted. My sponsor and his friend had both earned their fair share of first place trophies at various archery contests. The two typically equipped themselves with very high-tech bows. They provided me with a less fantastic model that more than met my beginner's needs. I was used to seeing the two hit bull's-eyes, even at the farthest ranges. My technique was simple. I just sort of aimed my bow, judging elevation as best I could, and then let loose my arrow with little more than a hope and a prayer. This day, however, was a little odd...I could already feel a certain magic in the air as we entered the animal target course. Mock-up targets, crafted to resemble various forest animals, were positioned along the walking paths through the woods. Each shooting location was marked with the corresponding range to the target. As we worked our way through the targets, we eventually came to the moose target. This target was positioned 80 yards from the shooting spot and far beyond my ability to accurately aim. On this ninth day of June, I got a little help. I didn't need the fancy calibrated sights that my sponsor and friend had. I didn't need the years of archery training. I had something better—a little bit of divine intervention. I raised my bow up, tried to judge the direction and elevation as best I could, and then set my arrow free. Eighty yards later, the arrow struck its mark, perfectly hitting the moose with an ideal shot in the small "bull's-eye" section marked upon the target. I was amazed. My sponsor asked if I'd like to shoot again, but I politely declined. The two pros then took their positions and each emptied their entire quivers—not a single arrow hit the target. The two hunters seemed confused as the arrows would fly, seemingly on course, and then a breeze or other phenomena would mysteriously deflect their arrows over, under, or to the side of the target. I remarked that perhaps some form of force field was protecting the target. We slowly walked up to the target, my sponsor and friend still shaking their heads in disbelief; and I pulled the one and only arrow out of that moose target, exclaiming, "I guess this means I'm good at moose hunting." The miracle was complete.

Amidst these huge and undeniable signs, there continued a steady stream of minor miracles. Songs with special meaning to me would pop on the radio, and right at their beginnings, at the moment I turned on my radio. Special clips appeared on television, and there were many significant dreams along with other motivational happenings. Independently, all were totally explainable. Together, they formed a volume of miraculous wonder. Someone was looking out for me.

Since I had to make up a class during Summer Academics, I lost all but 5 days of my scheduled summer leave. I was intent on making the most of what I had. After completing the whirlwind three weeks of Summer Academics, I rolled right into Survival, Evasion, Resistance, and Escape (S.E.R.E.) training. After S.E.R.E. was my "CONUS" Field Trip to Blytheville AFB, Arkansas, and

Little Rock AFB, Arkansas. While not the most exciting locations, it was still a thrill to visit operational Air Force bases and get some tours and briefings related to the missions they accomplished. One of the highlights was an air refueling mission where we got to refuel several FB-111s.

With most of my summer vacation spoken for, I did finally get home to New York on July 21st. A highlight of the trip was receiving an autographed photo of Dorothy Hamill. I can hardly describe the joy that filled my heart when I finally had the opportunity to open it. (Too precious to risk another trip through the mail, the autographed note had long been awaiting my return home).

On July 24th, I went into the City to spend some time with my brother; and we visited a number of Moose Hunting targets. The first place we visited was the New York City Public Library. This visit was to commemorate our 1982 visit where we searched through countless British Columbia phone books, looking for any and every Dudoward that appeared in print. From the library, we continued on to visit several sites of interest and some book stores. Then, just by luck, we happened to stray into Grand Central Station. I thought it would be an interesting place to explore. While there, my brother pointed out a rack with various train schedules as we passed by. When John casually mentioned that they had the schedules for Connecticut, along with his list of other places, I stopped in my tracks. After a brief conversation, John knew exactly where my mind was going. We went over to the schedules rack and I grabbed a schedule for trains to Riverside, Connecticut—Dorothy's hometown. Plans for a grand Moose Hunt were already formulating in my mind. We continued on, got some pizza for lunch, and went to the Museum of Broadcasting where we checked out the "Wide World of Sports 15th Anniversary" show. I reveled in the brief segment on Dorothy Hamill set to

"Somewhere Over the Rainbow." From the museum, we went on to Chinatown, looked around a bit, and eventually made our way to the World Trade Center. After a wonderful time hanging out with my brother on top of the world (or at least the City), we returned to Penn Station and made our traditional pass by the Dorothy Hamill poster outside of Madison Square Garden. We even retraced our steps, as best we could, from our February 12th, 1984, adventure to see Dorothy skate with Ice Capades. Satisfied with a great day, it was time to head below to catch a train for home and bid farewell to my wonderful brother. A few days later, I spent my last day at home, Dorothy's birthday, reflecting on a spiritually strong few days of re-centering on my home field. It is important to mention, on my flight back to Colorado, I opened up the United Airlines Magazine and was pleasantly surprised to see an article about Vancouver, Canada. I took note. I always do. Upon my return to the Academy, I started up in the Soaring program and ultimately got my glider wings after flying solo in the sailplane. I felt very proud. Silently soaring above the Academy, with beautiful mountains surrounding, was a blissfully remarkable experience. My success in gliders only increased my appetite for powered flight.

In the realm of spiritual refinement, I sought to pick up where I had left off. It was not practical to conduct an official battle the summer before, while in Basic Training, nor while transitioning into the Hell of my 4th Class year at the Academy. I was eager, in the Summer of 1985, to resume the tradition of conducting an anniversary battle to commemorate August of '82. With few exceptions, I continued to honor this tradition throughout the many years that followed. I had no photos of Valerie to post upon my cork bulletin board, as I did for Dorothy; but even without the pictures, there was never any doubt that I would always remember and cherish she who inspired me during my darkest days. All the inspiration I needed was safely kept within my heart. Even as I conducted my anniversary battle, I was planning an even larger effort—a record-breaking 100-day battle to lead me to what would be the greatest Moose Hunt ever. To that date, my record battle was 65 days. "The Great War of the Knight" would take me through to Christmas day and set the stage for the greatest Moose Hunting adventure I had ever embarked upon.

Around this same time, I also began to feel some inner conflict. There was a girl, a female cadet, who had caught my eye. I liked her. However, any thoughts put towards this girl seemed to pull me away from where my heart told me my true focus should be. I became very confused. Part of me wanted to withdraw deeper within, yet another part of me longed for some kind of companionship. Was this whole episode a test or was I merely overthinking things? I knew I needed to keep my loyalty strong for my ladies; and I still felt the warmth that this love provided—the love that had saved me, time and time again, from falling into the traps so often set along the path of young men.

With no shortage of emotional turmoil and occasional doubts, and amidst the backdrop of continued academic woes, I continued to find solace within my faith. My "world" was a safe harbor. Often times, in my diary, I would refer to this spiritual refuge as a separate world, apart from the cruelty and coldness that marred the landscape of what some choose to call "the real world." Who is to say what is real and what is not?

As the fall of 1985 progressed, I found inspiration developing plans for my Moose Hunt to Dorothy's hometown. Historically, Christmas has been the big event in December. My hopes and dreams were focused on the 26th and 27th of the month. From the small confines of my shared dorm room in Cadet Squadron Fifteen, I finalized my plans. I made hotel reservations from the communal phone booth down the hall. Months of reading and researching were converted into a target list that filled the pages of a small Moose Hunting notebook. The notebook would become my guide for the pilgrimage. Each chosen site had a special tie to Dorothy.

With my knightly passion growing, I knew it was time to make a very important purchase. It was time to acquire a sword! A real sword. With the assistance of my roommate and some friends, on December 7th we drove to the Citadel Mall where I found a beautiful sword that closely resembled the sword held by my knight statue back home; the one I got in Spain. We then drove to a packaging store where they wrapped, boxed and shipped my sword back to New York so that it would arrive, with plenty of time to spare, for Christmas. The packing store told me it should get there within the week. This is a significant point to note, as will later become evident. But for now, amidst my chivalrous euphoria, I had to keep my focus locked on the seven tough final examinations that were rapidly approaching—unfortunately, they were scheduled in a brutal back-to-back sequence. I failed one of my early finals, resulting in an overall failing grade for the class and guaranteeing my second year without a summer vacation. Despite all, I tried not to lose my focus on what was important in life. Knowing that any more "F"s would result in an automatic disenrollment, however, created a rather large mental burden. Despite all, I finally made it through finals; and I was back home in New York on the 21st of December. Upon my arrival, I became immediately concerned. I was short one very important Christmas gift. The sword that I was expecting to be waiting for me was nowhere to be seen—it was lost.

On December 23rd, I visited New York City with my brother. While there, I did some Moose Hunting. We visited Grand Central Station and picked up a current train schedule. We also visited the Public Library, site of our 1982 phone book excursion. Beyond hitting the Moose Hunting targets, we also enjoyed some of the beauty of classic New York City holiday sites. We stopped by to see the Christmas tree at Rockefeller Center and ascended the Empire State Building to view the city lights from above. Our final stop was, of course, the Dorothy Hamill poster outside of Madison Square Garden. It was a wonderful day out on the town with my brother!

On Christmas Day, I completed the 100th day of my spiritual battle, completing a purification effort that cleared the way for my greatest adventure ever.

December 26, 1985. It was a very cold and cloudy winter morning. I woke up at 6:35 am and quickly readied myself for the journey to come. I typically prefer not to eat on mornings where I travel, but I made an exception in this case and rapidly polished off an egg and toast. I knew it would be a long day and I wasn't sure when my next meal would come. Minutes later, I was in our car being driven to the Great Neck Train Station, along with my brother. We didn't have to wait long before the Long Island Rail Road train pulled into the station, and my brother and I were off on the opening leg of the adventure. While John would not accompany me on my grand Moose Hunt, he had agreed to help get me to the appropriate launching point at Grand Central Station. After that, I was on my own. At 8:40 am, I hopped a train on the New Haven line towards my destination in Connecticut. I quickly drifted into my own magical world as I watched the gray winter scenery flash by. My heart filled with excitement when I finally reached Riverside, Connecticut, at 9:37 am. The train ride had taken us through Rye, NY where, as a child, Dorothy would often go for morning skating practice. Needless to say, this detail was not lost on me.

Coming off the train, duffle bag in hand, I felt a little disoriented. I wasn't even aware that I was slowly meandering down the street where Dorothy's childhood home stood. My first objective was to find my way to the hotel where I had made reservations. It didn't take me long to get my bearings and, shortly thereafter, I arrived at the Greenwich Sheraton where, at 10:12 am, I checked in, dropped off my bag, and set off on my ambitious Moose Hunting pilgrimage.

Dorothy Hamill's old home, Riverside, Connecticut

My first target was obvious—172 Riverside Avenue—Dorothy's old house. I set out with my special green shirt and green striped socks. It should be no surprise that I wore my blue windbreaker and a baseball hat. As discretion is the better part of valor, I wisely chose to layer my winter coat over my windbreaker. At 15 degrees Fahrenheit (wind chill below zero), it was going to be quite the physically taxing adventure. I could feel the magic as I approached Dorothy's house. The modestly beautiful white home fit very naturally within this upper-middle-class suburban neighborhood. I slowed my pace and pulled my camera out of the case. Not wanting to attract too much attention, I didn't dwell for an extended period of time. I took several photographs and lingered long enough to lovingly reflect upon the significance of what I was experiencing. I could envision a young girl, waking well before her classmates, wearily climbing in her mother's car for a long drive to a practice rink. Where did she find the inspiration to continue this exhausting routine? It was hopes and dreams that inspired her. I could identify with this kind of passion. And then, years later, looking out from that front window and seeing crowds of adoring fans, all wanting to get a glimpse of the Olympic champion! Those things, and all the remarkable happenings in-between, happened right there! And so I stood, on that same spot, my soul filling—absorbing positive feelings and energy that I cannot adequately describe. I could feel the magic in the air—there was no doubt that I had crossed the bridge into my world. I was ready for more and there was much more to see.

After my first target, I prepared for many miles of walking. In total, I walked the equivalent of a marathon during my adventure; and I walked at a very quick pace, stopping only occasionally to take photos and to reflect upon the meaning of the special places I visited. There was no time for rest and no time for meals. I had a lot of ground to cover before darkness fell. The first day, I spent 6 hours battling the elements; and my legs grew tired and sore. My spirit, however, soared. I was walking the same streets that Dorothy walked, seeing the same sites that were part of her everyday life for so many years. It was special. It was magical.

On my first day, I visited Dorothy's elementary school, then her Junior High School and High School. Following the schools, I had quite a long journey to reach "The Dorothy Hamill Skating Rink," which I hit at half-past two. The rink was several hours from the hotel; and I knew it'd be a long, cold, walk back. I was anxious to return before it got too dark. I finally arrived back at the hotel at 4:20 pm, cold and tired. I had been pushing my limits all day so that my photography efforts would not be overcome by darkness—a real problem considering the shortest day of the year was less than a week before. However, I had one more Moose Hunting target to hit before I could call it a day—Caldor's. I had read in Dorothy's biography that this was the department store where she had purchased her first pair of skates. I knew I had to see it. I managed to snap a few photos using what little natural light remained in the day. Inside the store, I was pleasantly surprised to see that they still sold ice skates. I didn't buy any skates, but I did purchase a pack of Lifesavers—it was the least I could do. By the time I made it back to my hotel, it was already pitch dark outside. I was starving. Fortunately, the Greenwich Sheraton had an attached Chinese restaurant. My tired legs thanked me. I will always remember this as one of the best meals I've ever had. I ordered wonton soup, an egg roll, and chicken lo mein. The servings were much larger than I had anticipated; but after my icy day of adventuring across many miles, my stomach was more than capable of putting it all away. Delicious! The fortune from my fortune cookie stated: "You are filial, kind and trustworthy." I'd later tape it to my diary. My dinner was over at 6:15 pm, and I returned to my room under a lovely full moon. There was still some magic left in the day. As I collapsed upon my hotel bed and tuned the television to the hotel's only movie station, I was amazed to see that I was just in time for the beginning of the movie *Camelot*. I knew this could not be a coincidence. It was yet another sign—a miracle! Following the movie, I felt at total peace. I quickly fell asleep.

I woke early the next morning and carefully suited up, once more, in my defiant armor (blue windbreaker and baseball cap). I waited for the sun to rise and then headed out for the Riverside Yacht Club where Dorothy used to go swimming during her childhood summers. I arrived there just in time to see the old attendant raising the flag. I saluted the flag as it went up. On my return to the hotel, I made a final stop by Dorothy's house. Such a special place —I just had to spend a little more time there and say a proper farewell.

I returned to the hotel at 8:55 am and packed my bag before saying an emotional farewell to Room 202. The snow was starting to fall as I slowly made my way back to the Riverside train station. It was beautiful. Everything was beautiful. I arrived at the station at 9:40 am and caught the 10:11 train back to New York. The significance of this whole experience finally began to sink in during the peaceful return ride. After arriving at New York's Grand Central Terminal, I made the transfer to get myself over to Penn Station. From there, I was in familiar territory—a thirty-five-minute eastbound ride on the LIRR's Port Washington Line and I'd be home —almost. Once in Great Neck, I still had a half-hour walk ahead of me before my journey would truly be complete. By the time I arrived at my house, I was truly exhausted. I first returned to my room, closed my door, and drew the sword from my knight statue. I said a heartfelt and solemn thanks, expressing my great gratitude for the wonderful adventure I had just been blessed with. After this, I went to the kitchen to get some lunch. I was incredibly hungry, as you might imagine. I ate quite a lot. Even with my adventure complete, I still felt a special magic in the air. As I went to empty my garbage, I noticed some brown grocery sacks in the cupboard, one which had an advertisement for Ice Capades on the side. Interesting. Finally, after cleaning up from lunch, I collapsed upon the worn green sofa in our living room. The sofa sat right in front of our large picture window. My body had been pushed to the limit over the past several days and was wont for some recuperation time. I quickly fell asleep. When I awoke, about an hour and a half later, I saw my brother staring out the window. He had an astonished look upon his face. He said "Dave, look! Look out the window!" I did, but I didn't see a thing. "Sit up and look!" he urged more strenuously. I did, and I still didn't see anything at first. Then I glanced down upon our porch. A rather large rectangular box had been deposited as I slept. I knew it could be only one thing. My sword had arrived! There was no sign of a deliveryman and no signature was ever requested. My brother and I shared that special moment in complete awe. Perhaps I had finally earned it? Perhaps this was Heaven's way of saying thank you—thank you for keeping the faith. Thank you for being a true knight. This miracle, and the adventure that preceded it, are blessings I have never forgotten. I never will. In classic David Lange style, I collected all maps and mementos from my great adventure and carefully preserved them in a folder for all times.

Me with my sword, December, 1985

Even with the completion of this historic adventure, my Christmas vacation Moose Hunting was not at an end. I watched Dorothy skate on television, in a professional's figure skating competition, and on December 30th took another trip into the city with my brother. Besides some of the old places, we also visited the Manhattan "Sky Rink" where Dorothy frequently skated in the past. We had a large number of stops on our visit to The Big Apple, many of them with very special significance.

As the year closed, I organized my thoughts and writings. I created several tapes to bring back with me that included audio recordings of all the Dorothy Hamill interviews I had taped off of the television. I reflected upon an eventful year. I also fondly remembered the several magical days in Connecticut where I truly felt like I was venturing in another world.

I was not looking forward to my return to USAFA and "reality," but there was a part of me that knew this was the path I was meant to travel. I knew I'd be returning to my magical world before long.

My spring semester, sophomore year, was little better than the semester before. I put everything I had into trying to stay one step ahead of the Dean, yet my efforts often seemed futile; and I remained, perpetually, on the precipice of academic disenrollment. I never left the Academy grounds, as all my free time was channeled into academic survival. It was a battle in the truest sense. While I fought an internal battle to maintain the highest level of purity, consistent with my chosen calling, I also waged a very brutal external battle to survive the obstacles USAFA continued to place in my path. My vision remained focused, always, on a Graduation Day that I truly thought I might never see.

April 19, 1986. A note in my diary and little more. Amidst all the confusion and chaos, my weekend walk carried me past a car with a British Columbia license plate. What was that doing at the Academy? What, indeed. Perhaps it was a much-needed sign and a reminder of where my heart's focus needed to be? While my summer vacation was lost, yet again, a summer military training program would, quite unexpectedly, bring me closer than I had ever been to realizing a dream.

Summer programs, "Ops Air Force." On June 22nd, I arrived at McChord Air Force Base in Washington after a grueling day of travel and associated stomach issues. Our air travel took us to Travis AFB, California, followed by Norton AFB, California, and, eventually, to McChord AFB. Between flights, we were kept on board our C-141 aircraft for hours, with the temperature over 100 degrees Fahrenheit inside. Between the challenging day of travel and the 3:50 am wakeup, I was fairly exhausted by the time we reached our Visiting Airman Quarters at McChord. However, I should have known that my trials might be leading me towards yet another adventure when, on television that night, I saw a Mutual of Omaha Wild Kingdom show featuring the moose. A sign?

Further good news came when we were told we'd be getting to take a trip to Japan during our visit. Along with my classmates, I was very excited—most of us had never been to Japan. Better still, when I visited the Recreation Center, I discovered they were selling tickets for day trips up to Expo '86 in Vancouver, Canada. At last! This was finally my chance to get to visit British Columbia and bring myself that much closer to my Lady Valerie. I purchased a ticket for a trip, planning my visit prior to our projected departure for Japan. Everything seemed like it was coming together nicely. However, life is never that simple; and things worth having are never quite so easily acquired. My summer good news story quickly took a turn for the worse with an unfortunate accident that occurred while I was assigned to work with the Supply Squadron. My job, on this particular morning, was to shadow a young airman from the Supply Squadron and learn about that organization's contributions to the base's mission. The focus of the Operations Air Force program was to introduce cadets to the "real Air Force." My first day of introduction, June 24, 1986, was to be spent with the hard-working members of the Supply Squadron. I hopped in an Air Force blue pickup truck with the young airman I was shadowing, and we were off. One of our first tasks was to visit an office that was divesting itself of a multi-hundred-pound, multi-drawer safe. I took one look at the safe and knew we had no business trying to move that monster. I voiced my opinion on the matter. Clearly wanting to be rid of the behemoth, one of the civilians who worked in the office offered to help me and the airman carry the safe out to our truck and load it on the flatbed. Even with three of us on the job, I still thought it was a very bad idea. I went along with the plan, anyway. As we reached the truck, all three of us using all our might to slowly lift it up into the flatbed, our civilian helper gave out a yelp and shouted, "I'm out," leaving the safe to just two of us. It was more weight than we could carry. The metallic bone crusher dropped like a rock. Unfortunately, the corner of the safe landed squarely on my right foot. The foot instantly went numb, and I knew I was in trouble. The Airman quickly got me to the base clinic where x-rays were taken. The x-rays confirmed that my foot had been smashed—fractured in multiple places. They later transported me to the Army hospital where a doctor constructed a large plaster cast around my foot.

On a somewhat humorous note, when I woke up the next morning, I noticed a rather large blood stain upon my cast—my blood had soaked through the half-inch thick plaster cast. I knew this was not a good thing. The Army doctor who had tended to my foot the day before did have a rather difficult time getting the bleeding to stop. I was driven back to the hospital for a follow-up. In classic Army medicine style, the doctor looked at my blood-stained cast and determined that cutting the cast open wasn't something he wanted to do. He asked if I had a pencil and I provided him one. The Army doc drew an outline around the bloodstain and told me that if the stain grew any larger, after another day, then I should return and he'd cut open the cast and take a look. Wonderful.

Back at McChord AFB, our Academy Liaison Officer informed me that he'd have to send me back to USAFA because there was no way I could carry on with the trip while I was hobbling around on crutches. I was devastated—all those wonderful plans, and the dreams of what could have been, flashed before my eyes. More than anything, I felt crushed by losing an opportunity to go to Vancouver. I objected strongly and insisted that I could make the trip. The Lieutenant Colonel in charge, after calling back to check in with the Academy, told me that if I could be rid of the crutches before our flight to Japan then I would be allowed to continue. It was a tall order, but I agreed to the stipulations.

The next day, the 25th, I spent speed-crutching all around the base, chasing after the fast-moving squadron commander I was shadowing as he darted from one meeting to the next at break-neck speeds. My unconditioned hands were getting torn to shreds from the constant friction against the crutch grips. Things seemed to move from bad to worse when I learned that our trip to Japan had been moved up. This not only put into question my ability to get off the crutches, but it also knocked out my Vancouver trip. I defiantly swore an oath that one day, somehow, I would still make my pilgrimage to Vancouver.

While it would make for lovely fiction to claim that some sort of medical miracle cured me of my ailments, I believe it was simply a matter of pure blood and guts determination that permitted me to shuck my crutches in favor of a walking cast only a day prior to our departure for Japan. With a simple exclamation of "look, I can walk," I was cleared to move forward with the rest of the cadets to Japan.

While in Japan, we had a wonderful time. Basing out of Yokota Airbase, Japan, we were assigned to a C-130 airlift squadron. With a flying squadron as our host, we were blessed with an opportunity to fly all around the Pacific, visiting South Korea, Iwo Jima, as well as other bases in the area. Flying up in the cockpit, and on headset, was a remarkably motivating experience for me. As a military history major, my visit to Iwo Jima, and the historical island tour we took there, was nothing less than spectacular. However, I almost slid off the edge of Mount Suribachi when my walking cast lost its grip as I was gazing over the edge of the cliff, envisioning waves of Marines pouring in to take the island from the Japanese, back in World War II. I literally fell to my chest with my head at the edge of the cliff. I slowly crawled back away from the edge and then resumed my visualization while several shocked cadets looked on in horror. The time spent in Japan was revitalizing for me. On the 7th of July, we had another early morning with a 2:00 am wake-up for a flight through Alaska and back to McChord AFB, Washington.

While my chances for an orientation flight in a fighter-trainer jet waned, I realized there was time enough for one final shot at Vancouver. The crossroad I encountered was an either/or proposition—I could take my trip to Vancouver and give up the chance for a T-33 jet flight or I could stick around and, perhaps, get a flight. I had never been on a jet incentive flight. It was something I had dreamed of doing for many years. This was really big stuff! But this desire, as powerful as it was, could not match the passion deep within my heart to travel north into Canada. I gave up the opportunity for a flight and purchased tickets to head up to Expo '86. I hoped and prayed that my schedule would not shift again. Thanks be to God, it did not.

On July 9, 1986, I hopped the bus departing from our base for the ride up to Vancouver and the Expo '86 fairgrounds. It was the most magical day. Everything was beautiful—truly beautiful. I limped about the grounds in a dreamy state. The fair was spectacular, but I felt an incredible magic in the air. I felt so at peace. I was half expecting Valerie to round any corner, and I was so sure she had been there before. Perhaps she was there that day? Regardless, the moose was close and leading me thoughtfully through this magical experience. I purchased several mementos while there which I still cherish. I wear the holographic unicorn pendant each August. The unicorn: a symbol of strength through purity of heart and soul! Ticket stubs, maps, and even my Canadian pocket change are lovingly protected within a folder I made to hold these treasures. The day belonged to Valerie. And, with August coming, it was appropriate to pay proper homage to she who saved me from myself but four years before. I didn't see Valerie that day...yet I did. She was there with me, and I could feel it. I boarded the return bus that evening with a true feeling of peace inside my heart.

Collectibles from my Expo '86 trip to Vancouver, B.C., Canada

I never did get a jet incentive ride on my Ops Air Force trip but; somehow, it really didn't seem to matter in the face of my miraculous journey to Vancouver. We returned to the Academy on July

12th; and I completed my summer by training Basic Cadets how to shoot, as a Combat Arms Training and Maintenance (CATM) instructor. With August, of course, a new anniversary battle began; and I felt the winds of fortune change as my head returned to a very good place. I could definitely feel some magic in the air, and I knew I was not alone. I had hardly begun "The Great Battle of Four Pillars" when, on August 2nd, while walking through the woods in broad daylight, four large owls swept across my path. I had never seen one in the wild before. Four owls and four years from the day I first met Valerie. How could I not take note? Yes, the magic was returning. I could only hope I could sustain the passion through yet another school year.

My battles with the Dean continued. Yet so, too, did my Moose Hunting adventures. Borrowing my roommate's car or renting my own, I began to increase the range of my adventures—the Colorado Springs/Denver area was rich with targets. These adventures, likewise, were not devoid of accompanying "coincidences" that helped both to restore and build my faith. Despite all of this positive energy, maintaining a high level of enthusiasm and inspiration within the context of my Academy experience was never an easy thing. The Academy took every bit of energy I had. Late nights, early mornings, and weekends were devoted, nearly entirely, to catching up with my studies. Though challenges and disappointments continued to plague me, I fought hard to keep my thoughts focused on positive things. When I describe all the "battles" we fight in life, I am really talking about the internal struggle we all face to overcome the difficulties and negative thoughts that creep into our minds and to fight to keep a positive outlook and to appreciate the blessings of each and every day. It's not easy—it's a fight. I understood this struggle at an early age but "understanding" and "overcoming" are two different matters altogether.

I wanted to fly. During my graduation flight physical, I was dealt a very painful blow. I was informed that I was no longer pilot qualified. Once again, it seemed as if my dream to fly was slipping out of reach. There was only one thing I could do—keep on keeping on. And that's what I did. Much to my joy, I managed to pass the infamous "red lens test" several weeks later; and I regained my pilot qualification status. Shortly thereafter, we won the Softball Wing Championship (I coached the team and, of course, contributed as a player). Not very long after that, my New York Mets won the World Series. Not to be outdone, the New York Giants won the Super Bowl in January of 1987, defeating the local favorite Denver Broncos. Academics aside, it was a good fall. One by one, I overcame the Academy's challenges. Water Survival, dreaded since before I even enrolled as a cadet—victory! My final Cadet Fitness Test—best score ever—victory! My most challenging course load ever—victory!

And throughout all this, the small miracles continued. Seemingly growing in number, they comforted me and reminded me that I was not alone on the journey. Even as I celebrated Valerie and the early "War Years," during my final August as a cadet, I was reminded that inspiration comes in many forms. Not to be forgotten, the "other woman," Ms. Dorothy Hamill, would make a reappearance.

On August 21, 1987, the Fourth Classmen (freshmen) erroneously delivered the wrong newspaper to our room. Instead of his regular paper, my roommate received the Rocky Mountain News. As I had some time on my hands before the afternoon Retreat Ceremony, I decided to take a look through the paper. As I read, I stumbled upon an eye-catching, full-page advertisement for an upcoming "Stars on Ice" show. Gracing the ad was a large photo of Dorothy. I was thrilled! Dorothy would be in Denver in September! I had waited three years, hoping that she might return to the Colorado area to skate. It seemed to me that this must be a sign. Somehow, I knew I must try to get tickets and the required approvals to leave the Academy grounds. Immediately after the Retreat Ceremony, I rushed inside, grabbed the phone in our squadron telephone room, and called to order my ticket for the best seats that were available. Literally, as I got off the phone, I looked outside and saw two brilliant and absolutely beautiful rainbows arcing through the sky. I felt a huge surge of energy within my heart. I then knew that these happenings were more than just a fortunate coincidence. This was a sign.

The big day, September 25, 1987, came soon enough. I had to get special permission to leave that Friday night because we had scheduled military training the next day. The request I submitted worked its way up through our cadet chain of command to our Air Officer Commanding, Major Atkins. I suspect it went up with some amplifying remarks from friends. Many years later, a retired Colonel Atkins mentioned how he remembered I had a crush on Dorothy Hamill. My request was approved. The path was now clear for my next great adventure. There were still a few loose ends to tie up.

Since I did not own a vehicle, I had to work a transportation plan for my trip up to Denver. In this regard, I got lucky. One of my good friends worked on the Cadet Group Staff and was not required to remain in the Cadet Area prior to our training day. In fact, he had already planned on heading up to Denver that Friday night for a date with his girlfriend. He agreed to drop me off at the ice show and then pick me up after it was over. I was very grateful for this offer.

With transportation secured, I turned my attention to my final piece of preparation. Several days before, I had ordered eleven long stem roses from the Cadet Florist Shop so that I might throw them on the ice after Dorothy skated, as I had seen done following

Olympic performances. The eleven roses signified each year since Dorothy had won the Olympics. That afternoon, I picked up the flowers and prepared for the outing. I was very excited!

At 4:18 pm, I signed out at the Squadron CQ Desk. I had my camera and roses in hand. Naturally, I was wearing my windbreaker, baseball cap, and my lucky green Moose Hunting shirt (the one that had been to Riverside with me and on so many other Moose Hunting adventures). My friend picked up his date on the way, and they dropped me off at McNichols Sports Arena at 6:21 pm. I had some time, once I reached my seat, to check my camera and put in my 1000 ASA film. I wasn't taking any chances. I knew the venue would be dimly lit and the very light-sensitive film would better permit me to shoot skaters in motion during the performances. Although the show was scheduled to begin at 7:30 pm, the producers decided to delay the start until 7:45 pm to accommodate late arriving guests who were having to deal with some very bad traffic conditions on the way in.

"Stars on Ice" was a fantastic production. The show included many terrific skating stars: Dorothy, of course, and Scott Hamilton, Lea Ann Miller and Bill Favver, Toller Cranston, Kathleen Schmelz, Judy Blumberg and Michal Seibert, Brian Pockar, Rosalyn Sumners, Barbara Underhill and Paul Martini, to name a few. Dorothy had a number of appearances which, naturally, filled my heart with joy. However, each time I got ready to toss my flowers on the ice after her performance, the lights went dark and the spotlight was turned off. I realized it would be silly to toss my flowers onto the pitch-black ice rink while Dorothy was already making her exit "off stage." Not only that, they would create a potential hazard for the skaters that followed. The show came and went—it was beautiful. And there I sat. As I reflected upon the wonderful evening of skating, I could not help but consider the fate of the eleven long stem roses still in my possession. Common sense would have dictated that I retreat with my flowers and make my way to the exit with the flow of the crowd. However, this was no ordinary evening and a Quixotic inspiration filled my heart. This passion drove me to execute one of the gutsiest moves I've ever made. I reversed course, walking against the flow of humanity traveling towards the exits, and made my way down to the entrance of the backstage area. Blocking the door was a man screening people for press passes or backstage access passes. Anyone without a pass was getting turned away. Against my better judgment, I waited, and watched, and looked for an opportunity. And then it came! While the guard was facing the other direction, fully engaged turning someone else away, I quickly darted past him to the backstage area. At this point, I could see my entire cadet career flash before my eyes. Was I now a criminal? Would this mean disenrollment from USAFA, should I be arrested and prosecuted? I did not dwell long upon these questions although I could feel the adrenaline coursing through my body.

I found myself backstage with a group of elites, awaiting the stars to emerge from the dressing room. Among the group waiting were some stars in their own right—skaters Jill Trenary, Karen Kadavy, and I believe I even saw Debbi Thomas. Since this event had been the tour's opening show, there were a lot of other big names there to see it. I patiently waited amidst this group, a little nervous that I might be ferreted out. My mouth grew very dry, and I tried not to make eye contact with any of the security guards wandering about. And then, finally, like a dream, Dorothy came out. She was with her husband and the two were pushing through the crowd, obviously trying to make a hasty departure. I knew I had to be quick. I pushed on into the crowd and tried to set an intercept course. One of the security personnel came up to me and stopped me. She saw that I had some flowers to present, and she said she'd take them to Dorothy. I would have no part of this. I politely told her that I wanted to present them myself. This is when things really got magical. Dorothy saw me, looking up towards her and trying to reach her with my flowers. I'm sure I must have had a "please, Dorothy" look in my eyes when our eyes met. At this point, she pushed her way through the crowd and over to where I was stopped. Her smile was beautiful. I handed her the roses, shook her hand, and told her how much I loved the show. I also thanked her for being an inspiration. Then, to my amazement and joy, she pulled me in and gave me a hug and kissed me on my left cheek. It wasn't just a quick peck but a beautiful and genuine kiss. I was in Heaven! Again, I thanked her and she thanked me and gave me a friendly wave goodbye as she made her way out. For years, I had fantasized about such things. Finally, my dream came true. It was a magical moment in time. For a short span, I remained in place, my heart peacefully floating amidst the heavenly clouds of my own little world, while Dorothy made her way out of the stadium. Finally, I turned to make my way out, as well. On my way, I met up with Scott Hamilton and I congratulated him, as well, for a terrific show. I shook Scott's hand and got him to sign the cover of my program. Sometimes, I wonder if, perhaps, I should have asked Dorothy to sign my program. I know she would have. But, no—the moment was perfect just as it was. It wasn't about photo opportunities or autographs—it was about saying thank you to someone who inspired me, someone who made a difference in my life.

At 10:34 pm, I departed the area and met up with my friend, Mark, and his date. They jokingly asked if I got to meet Dorothy. Both were silent, in awe, when I told my story. After dropping off his date, Mark and I returned to the Academy, just after midnight. I hastily wrote down my story within my diary while it was still fresh within my mind. I went to bed, feeling completely at peace. There was, of course, no way I was going to fall asleep. I think I finally got three hours of shuteye before I woke the next morning. When I did, there was already a note posted on our squadron's information whiteboard that "Dave Lange got hugged and kissed by Dorothy Hamill last night." My fan status was well known within the squadron, and I knew all the guys would be very happy for me. What a great adventure!

Dorothy Hamill performing in Stars on Ice, McNichols Sports Arena, Denver, Colorado (September 25, 1987)

A powerful autumn followed with increasing reminders of Valerie. Through challenging academics and T-41 (a military version of the Cessna 172 aircraft) powered flight training, the beautiful coincidences continued—special songs brought back special memories. With a newly revised version of Steve Winwood's "Valerie" getting lots of airplay, it was clear to me that my focus must remain sharp. While fortune had blessed me to meet Dorothy and thank her, in person, I had yet to come anywhere near my long-standing life goal to find and thank

Valerie. Each play of "Valerie" on the radio reminded me of special days past and a vow yet unfulfilled. Even with the coming of winter, and the Olympic games, Valerie's presence increased within my thoughts and dreams.

Before long, the cold Colorado winter gave way to a warm and inviting spring at the Academy. I had overcome several medical challenges and finally received my Pilot Qualification (PQ) status. I would be going to pilot training after graduation! After seven semesters of peril, I finally felt in control of my destiny. In fact, I was still so paranoid about academics that I charged headlong into my final semester like a wild bull while many classmates were pulling back the throttles. When the dust settled, I was looking at an unbelievable 3.57 semester GPA. I had never broken 3.0. The ridiculous side to this story is that I earned a "Dean's Pin" for academic excellence. Because I earned it for that semester, I would have it for graduation; and it would be reflected in the graduation program. I really didn't feel like I should be wearing a Dean's Pin. After putting my parents through Hell for four years (they dreading a phone call saying I had been academically disenrolled), Mom wasn't having "any of that" when I said I wasn't going to wear the pin. So I, somewhat sheepishly, wore the Dean's Pin star on my uniform throughout all the Graduation Week events. In the end, I guess I really did earn it.

Grad Week was chock full of activities. Parades and ceremonies and a final chance to thank all the friends who helped get me through. It was a magical time. I was very fortunate to have Brigadier General (retired) Robert Lee Scott, Jr. (author of *God Is My Co-Pilot*) commission me. There's kind of a nice story related to that, too. My squadron Air Officer Commanding had written to General Scott earlier in the year and asked if he would be willing to come out to commission some of the members of the War Eagles Class of '88. He tentatively said yes. After I learned this, I read his book. I loved it. I was so excited and inspired that I wrote him a long letter telling him how much it meant to me that he was willing to come out for our commissioning ceremony. I didn't know it at the time but, apparently, General Scott was very close to backing out. He was getting up there in age (80 years old); and he wasn't convinced that it would be a good idea to travel from his home in Georgia to Colorado, especially as he had doubts about whether it would be meaningful to a bunch of young officer candidates. His friend and assistant wrote me a lovely letter in return. She told me that my letter had convinced him to make the trip. I was thrilled! On the morning of June 1st, 1988, General Scott swore me in at our squadron's commissioning ceremony.

Following the commissioning ceremonies, which each squadron held independently, it was time for the big show. For four very long years, an image had helped propel me through the darkness. The image was graduation day. A blue sky, a thousand of my classmates surrounding me, and the roar of the United States Air Force Thunderbirds overhead as a thousand white parade caps flew into the air. I never thought I'd make it. I thought that if I did, it would be raining, or I would be sick, or something. But June 1, 1988, was a beautiful day. The excitement was unbelievable as we formed up in the stadium tunnel and finally marched onto the field at Falcon Stadium. We took our seats, listened intently to the speeches, and then, one by one, were called across the stage to receive our diplomas and salute. We then exited via a couple of ramps, saluted our classmates, shook hands (or high fived!), and eventually made our way back to our seats. After a few more final words, the Commandant of Cadets uttered those words we had been dreaming of hearing for all those years—"Class of 1988, you are dismissed!" And then, just like in the dream, the Thunderbirds roared overhead and the caps went into the air. I believe my Parade Cap is still in orbit somewhere around the earth. To that point, Graduation Day was, without any doubt, the best day of my life! Cadet Lange was now Second Lieutenant Lange, and I felt proud to join the ranks of the world's greatest Air Force. The road had been very bumpy and perilous. I knew it was a journey I could not have made alone. I felt grateful.

United States Air Force Academy graduation photo (June 1, 1988)

Following graduation, my father and I drove back to New York from the Academy while my mother and sister flew back home. "The Foreign Campaign," the successor to the period in my life I called "The War Years," officially ended on June 3rd when I concluded "The Great Offensive" battle at 159 days. As was always the case, my spiritual journey was inextricably linked to my day-to-day existence. I had been tested as never before and, though worn and battle damaged, I emerged from the clouds of war with sword in hand and my honor fully intact. There was a peaceful feeling of closure to it all. At home, I gazed upon a note I had taped to the wall in my room—the message was a reminder that spiritual refinement was a never-ending struggle. My note read simply: "The war never ends, we just change battlefields." I knew great challenges lay ahead. However, even with this warning close at hand, I felt there was time enough for a brief pause to reflect upon a hard-fought victory. I wanted to catch my breath and take a moment to reflect, with satisfaction, upon the adversity I had faced and the obstacles I had overcome. It was appropriate to feel proud...and I was. My Academy yearbook quote captured the spirit:

When winds blow cold, and skies grow dark
And others turn to flee—
Ride forth brave knight with sword raised high
To claim the victory!

Chapter Eight

FAILURE ISN'T ALWAYS FAILURE

I had the opportunity, after graduation, for a wonderful trip to Ireland with my mother. Beyond that, I was anxious to get down to Texas to begin pilot training. To help expedite the timeline, I gave away half of my sixty days of graduation leave. While a cadet at the Academy, I had signed up for the first Undergraduate Pilot Training (UPT) class date available. I was itching to get my flying career started.

It was a hot and muggy July day when my father and I began our drive from New York down to Texas. After dropping my father off at the San Antonio Airport, I continued my trek down to Del Rio, Texas. The landscape soon turned barren. I believe this was the first time I actually saw real tumbleweeds. Looking for entertainment, I hit the scan button on my car radio. The digits spun and finally landed on a Spanish-speaking station. I hit the scan again—after a full cycle, the radio returned to the same station. I was in unfamiliar territory, and there were no reminders of my previous life in either New York or Colorado. On July 15, 1988, I reported for duty at Laughlin AFB, in Del Rio, Texas. My only motivation would be the smell of jet fuel and the sound of T-37 and T-38 aircraft engines.

My decision to begin pilot training at the earliest opportunity proved to be a disastrous miscalculation. I had completely underestimated how severely the Academy had burned me out. All too quickly, I realized that I had little energy left to devote to an incredibly challenging endeavor like Air Force Pilot Training. Added to this, I was frustrated to discover that over half my classmates had already memorized large volumes of the required-to-know "Warnings, Cautions, and Notes" from the T-37 Dash-One manual along with all the Emergency Procedures Boldface. Once again, I felt like the poorly networked guy who "failed to get the memo" about befriending a former (or present) Undergraduate Pilot Training (UPT) instructor pilot so that I could get the "gouge" required for a running start at training. Several students even had complete Xeroxed copies of the T-37 Dash One Flight Manual. This seemed very unfair. I was, once again, feeling like I was not competing on a level playing field. I was never a good memorizer so I reverted to my Academy ways. I would force myself to stay up as late as it took to get the required information loaded into my brain for the next day. I stayed up until midnight, each night, studying. This became a major problem considering that our pilot training showtimes were between 3:00 am and 3:30 am. I began each 12-hour workday in a veritable comatose state. Added to this, my First Assignment Instructor Pilot (FAIP) had signed on for so many additional duties that we never got to see him until it was actually time to fly. I was jealous of the other students who received engaged instruction throughout the day. So, each day, I headed out to fly under the hot Texas sun. Temperatures reached 120 degrees on the ramp and 140 degrees under the closed canopy of our Cessna T-37 training jet. It was no surprise that I got airsick and had trouble concentrating. Before I ever even got into the air, I was feeling exhausted and cooked alive. The result was inevitable —I was plagued by airsickness. There was a part of me that just wanted the pilot training experience to end. I fell behind before we had hardly even started. Yet, each day, I showed up, threw up, and struggled to learn a thing or two during the limited time my brain was focusing. My instructor gave up on me. Just as I was starting to overcome my air sickness, it became apparent he was trying a little too hard to give me the "option out"—six air sickness events and it's an automatic disqualification from flight training. I would not give him the satisfaction. On my 5th flight, he wrote me up for being "passively airsick." That means that I didn't throw up, but he was convinced that I was "not in the game" due to airsickness. I objected. Knowing that it would be a tough sell to disenroll me for a "passive airsickness event," on my 6th flight, he was courteous enough to ask me, at 10-minute intervals, how I was feeling. He knew only too well that if I answered, just once, that I was feeling "a little queasy," I'd effectively eliminate myself from the program. I politely responded "I'm fine," at each query. Unfortunately, blood and guts aside, I had fallen too far behind and was eventually eliminated from pilot training for not being able to progress at the required rate. My final mission was on the 27th of September and, with a strange shift in winds, I was seeing the local flying pattern from a direction I had never seen it before. My fate was sealed. It was the worst day of my life. It was the end of my dream of being a fighter pilot. I can still remember sitting alone, in the dark, in my flight commander's office, and waiting for him to arrive so that I might sign my final disenrollment paperwork. It was a sad and lonely time. Yet it was also a meaningful and reflective silence. I recalled the real reasons why I joined the Air Force, and I knew it was about much more than flying. The reasons were big and transcended any airframe or mission. When my flight commander arrived, he took instant pity upon me, sitting there in the dark; and he urged me to remain seated. However, I was intent on ending this experience in the same professional manner with which I began. I popped to attention and fired off my best salute, reporting in as a sharp officer should. I was not about to let adversity tarnish my professionalism. To stand tall in the face of failure—that's significant. Of the many positive and glowing performance reports I have received over the years, I still enjoy looking back upon a report which many would have burned or buried deep within some folder of useless paperwork. It's my training report from pilot training. The report is simple and to the point, but the final block has meaning for me: "Lt Lange displayed excellent military bearing throughout his training. He always maintained a positive attitude in spite of the difficulties he encountered. Lt Lange is an excellent junior officer and will be an asset to the Air Force." Over the years, I've seen too many people pitch out of the fight when things didn't go their way. That was never my style. The report, perhaps unintentionally, captured a fundamental quality that continues to drive me. I never enter a fight because I think I can win; I engage because the cause is just and the battle needs to be fought—my ability to "win" is irrelevant.

As I walked out of my flight commander's office, the next part of my Air Force career began. I knew that if I could overcome this shock and still keep my motivation to serve our country, that a whole new world of possibilities would unfold before me. While my flying didn't make the cut, my academic average at pilot training, nearly 97% on test scores, more than qualified me for a slot at Navigator School. However, a Nav School slot was far from a guarantee. In the interim, I was assigned on "casual status" to work at the Outbound Assignments Office at Laughlin AFB. In this capacity, I had the unenviable task of interviewing a number of my classmates who also washed out and typing up the appropriate paperwork to send to the Air Force Personnel Center so that the

Center might work their follow-on assignments. Several of these interviews were tearful ones, my classmates still suffering from the recent shock of a shattered life dream. It was difficult to relive my own experience through these encounters but, in the end, who better to show them the appropriate empathy and care than one of their own. I was there to help them through it, as best I could.

The experience of "washing out" of pilot training tested my professionalism. The devastating blow also provided a challenge spiritually. But I knew that faith is not about reward—it's about faith...and loyalty. I had to be strong and not let daily events weaken my faith. Very often, however, it is not our efforts that save our faith so much as it is our faith that becomes our salvation.

I was in need of an adventure, and October was always a good month for such quests. I was reading the book *Myths and Legends of the Middle Ages* which got me into the right mindset. On October 7th, I was off in search of the Moose once more. Following work, I made the long and boring drive to San Antonio where I planned to spend the night prior to my very early airline flight the next morning. I didn't sleep particularly well that night and, unfortunately, had to begin my travel day at 4:40 am. Thankfully, it was only a short drive from my hotel room to the airport. My day's journey would take me back to Colorado Springs, Colorado. While there, I joined up with my former roommate and his fiancé and we went to see the Air Force vs. Navy football game. Air Force won! After the game, I was off to the mall to purchase a replica Excalibur sword which had been on my mind for some time. The very next day, I drove with my new sword to the Broadmoor Hotel where, in a lot near the famous World Arena, I properly christened the weapon. In my diary, I note that the day was spectacularly beautiful. After performing my little sword ceremony, I went into the ice arena (leaving my sword back at the car, of course). At the entry was a poster for Nutrasweet National Ice Skating Month with Dorothy Hamill on it. Surely, this was a sign. Inside the arena, the spectacular moose painting still proudly hung. I spent several hours at the rink and walking around the lake at the Broadmoor. I could feel the spirit growing within my heart again. At the lake-side, I admired the fascinating journeys of a number of remote-controlled sailboats and had a lovely chat with a little girl about her techniques for feeding squirrels. I couldn't help but feel at peace, watching this precious little one innocently feed peanuts to all the hungry squirrels who came to call upon her. She was a part of what is good in this world.

After leaving the Broadmoor, I headed for the Academy and spent some time there reflecting upon the great battles of my cadet days. I wandered the grounds for a while, deep in thought. Eventually, I left and headed for the Chapel Hills Mall where I elected to visit a bookstore. The store also had a very small collection of VHS movies, and I was very pleasantly surprised (and yet not) to discover they had a copy of *Man of La Mancha*, a movie I had been searching for, for some time. I purchased this movie as well as *The Sound of Music*, which I have always associated with the '76 Winter Olympics in Innsbruck, Austria.

By and by, my Colorado adventure came to an end. It was, however, quite a fitting finale when, on my drive back to Laughlin Air Force Base from the San Antonio Airport, I heard John Denver's "Rocky Mountain High" on my car's radio. Nothing could have more perfectly put a bow on this terrific trip. It was a journey I was greatly in need of. My diary volume recounts how I watched *Man of La Mancha* in my dorm room and held several knight books close to my heart with some tears rolling down my cheeks. It felt good to be re-centered on who I was and what I believed in. How very appropriate that, several weeks later, I should begin a new War Game and also begin a new period in my life, "The Return to Arms," following on the heels of the Foreign Campaign. The time had come to return to the old ways. I had almost forgotten that life was a battle. My UPT failure was a shock, but it also drove me back home to those things that were most important to me—faith and the quest—Good over Evil!

November 6, 1988, had not been a great day; and I certainly had done little to merit any kind of help from above. Maybe that's why it came. The little reminders and small miracles that have made my life so special have also been my salvation. On the night of the 6th, I was watching television shows that I had previously recorded on a Video Cassette Recorder (VCR) tape. When I was finished, I hit the rewind button to rewind the VCR tape back to the start. The tape was spinning in the machine, as usual, but then it stopped in the middle of rewinding and started playing. Where it chose to stop was even more amazing. I looked towards my television set—the tape had stopped and then began playing Steve Winwood's "Valerie" video. Even more impressive—the replaying began from the very beginning of the song. I watched in complete awe and amazement. Surely, this was another one of God's gentle reminders. My Friends were helping me, yet again. I felt ashamed of my mental weakness—I had done absolutely nothing to deserve such beautiful messages and reminders. I felt unworthy of such divine intervention yet it came, all the same. I was grateful and I was moved. Several days later (November 10th), I found out that I was accepted for Navigator training with a report date of "on or before December 13th." I was given a second chance to make things right in my Air Force career just as I had been given another chance to make things right in my life. I rented and watched the movie *Excalibur* that night. I was back in the saddle and additional "coincidences" and small miracles followed which I will not recount here. I did as best a knight could to show my gratitude through vigils, song, and deed. Working in the Outbound Assignments Office, I was afforded the unique opportunity to be able to draft my own set of orders and rapidly get them signed by all the required offices. I was chomping at the bit to move on with my life.

Come December, it was time to take to the road and leave Del Rio, Texas behind me. Early in the morning, before the sun was up, I hopped in my Chevy S10 Blazer, popped in my Led Zeppelin tape, cranked up the volume, and roared out of town with "Ramble On" thundering through the speakers. I was happy to be done with this most recent misadventure, and I felt like I was driving towards my future. In days to come, I would learn an incredibly valuable life lesson. Sometimes, our greatest failures pave the way for our greatest successes. Some achievements are only made possible through strange twists of fate—departures from our chosen path that we may curse today, not understanding the divergence might well be the greatest gift imaginable. My pilot training failure exemplified this life lesson. My elimination from the program set the stage for some truly wonderful blessings—life events that would not have been possible had I taken a different path—the path I wanted at the time. The deviations we make in life set us on a course for all that is to come. Were I offered the opportunity, I would not change a thing. I am grateful for where my path has led me. I have faith that my path will lead me to where God intends that I should travel. The trip doesn't have to feel good and the destination may not always be what we had hoped for—but none of this matters. What's right is right. Looking beyond personal pain and anxiety and trusting—this is the essence of faith. Failure isn't always failure.

Chapter Nine

FLIGHT TRAINING

On December 3, 1988, I arrived in Sacramento, California for Specialized Undergraduate Navigator Training (SUNT). I moved into an apartment on the 6th and bought a copy of *Don Quixote* that same day—I knew I'd need the extra inspiration for the road ahead.

Shortly after starting up "nav training," we were granted Christmas leave; and I took the opportunity to return to New York for a very wonderful and highly reflective week. I could feel the magic return as I raced around town on my bicycle, visiting many special and "magical" spots that have provided me with inspiration across the years. I also spent lots of time looking through my old Moose Hunting files and, of course, reflecting upon spiritual matters at the park. While riding about the paved back playground area at Saddle Rock School, I could almost see Valerie still sitting there upon the stone steps that led up to the gymnasium. Like always, Valerie was watching out over her knight. This time, I envisioned her in a winter coat. My diary also recounts a rather unusual story that occurred while looking out upon the sea at my park. From my diary, January 1, 1989:

Today, I rode about and went to the park and other areas of strength. And, upon the same steps back at the school, I saw my lady as I did some years ago. No longer dressed in summer purple but with a winter coat. I rode about and sang aloud—faith is a wondrous thing. I could dismiss much but then I would have nothing save the miracles and miracles must add to faith, not be a foundation upon which it rests. No, today I sought out my lady and she was there—"to the park," said she, and there I rode with the speed of the wind (peddling up hills as fast as I could). Then, down I roared and charged the park—more laps and song and then to the waters. Northward, I turned. I briefly doubted my bearings then realized them true—I should not doubt. I sang aloud and the sea sang back. From across the shore, my lady smiled. If I could only reach her—"Oceans Away..."—I remember. Then, an idea —I would throw my kiss to her. I searched for a stick—and found one. I then kissed the stick and prepared to toss it across the sea. As I threw it, I heard a snap. I looked out to see my stick fall somewhere in the water—it did not. Ah yes, then it must have snapped and be lying behind me. I scoured the entire area but could not find it. It was like it had vanished in mid-air. So, you say—"sure Dave, nice story." Well, that's what I said at first but then I remembered a quote from Miracle on 34th Street. *It went, "Faith is believing when common sense tells you not to." And thus, I thought. Perhaps the stick really did reach my lady, somehow. No, not perhaps—my small token of appreciation made that great voyage and I do believe it did. Welcome to the World of David Lange—a world I've forsaken for too long. Let no man be my judge! I must believe and it must be with all my heart. A new year is here—let's correct the mistakes we have made before. Don't explain yourself to anyone or belittle your own thoughts. Speak and do as you believe—and believe in the magic—believe in the love and the wonder —believe in the Moose and your ladies—and believe in the Knight. Believe not for sake of belief—believe what you know to be true—it is true! I swear it is! Know it! Live it! Be it!"*

So went the day...and my entry to the new year. I had a very nice Christmas. I really enjoyed a terrific tackle football game during the break. But it was the inspiration and the power of faith that made the journey back home a remarkable and memorable one. My vivid Valerie dreams returned to me and, with them, a renewed sense of hope.

On the 21st of January, 1989, I recalculated the number of days since I had last seen Valerie; and this number returned as a regular part of each and every diary entry. In doing so, it felt like I found a part of myself that was lost. I also began to understand my environment and even wrote a great deal about the trials of being mired in the swamp, desperately fighting to reach the faint light of a distant shore. It was a hard fight, but I was understanding and dealing with my troubles in an effective way. On January 24th, I wrote:

And yes—Vancouver (as most probable locale) remains on my target list. Expo was merely an excursion into the magic land—I must return one day. Perhaps she is married—name changed; perhaps she has moved oceans away and none but a fantastic FBI investigation could locate her—but I shall not give up. Destiny will work things as they were meant to be—and all for a purpose—a good one.

On February 4th, after calling the public library in downtown Sacramento, I set forth upon an important Moose Hunt—seeking the most current phone directory for Vancouver. As I passed by an

"Alhambra Street," I could not help but smile—it was a gentle reminder of a brief but beautiful conversation with Valerie as we shared time together at the Alhambra Palace and Fortress in Granada, Spain. At the library, I was very pleased to find the current edition of the Vancouver phone book. Unfortunately, there was no Valerie Dudoward listed though I did take down the names of the four Dudowards I did find. It was such a long shot. Seven years after Spain, I was quite convinced that Valerie had likely gotten married and changed her name. Also, I never had any evidence that she had ever lived in Vancouver, in the first place. Still, these magical little trips helped to keep hope alive and bring me closer to my world. I also jotted down the phone number for the Office of Vital Statistics of British Columbia. If Valerie had married, then perhaps there might be some marriage records available through this public office. Whether or not they would grant me access was an entirely different matter. Mine was a dream that simply could not die. This quest had become too much a part of who I was, and I was unwilling to dig the grave—it would be my own.

Little signs and small miracles continued to inspire me. When there were no signs to guide or inspire, I kept up the good fight. I fought and fought and fought. In Nav School, I found great pleasure in flying our "Polaris" training profile which took us over Vancouver, B.C., Canada. In my heart, I felt that my Lady Valerie might be somewhere down there. My diary pages were filled with reflections. Here's just one, from April 17, 1989:

Within my heart, this evening, I feel a sense of sorrow—a sadness, an emptiness, but as I feel this within I also feel good inside because I know that it is my Lady Valerie whom I miss and the sadness is proof to me that my heart remains true. No, it's no story of fiction—it is reality, but a reality so divine that it takes on the beauty of a Fairy Tale. True now, as always before, I love Valerie with all my heart. But yet I regret each passing day—2,437 of them to this day—for each day seems to put time between us while I know not how to go about a countdown to zero, as I know not when, if ever, I may see dear Valerie again. I've so little to go on. Seven years ago, almost—I knew a name and I heard tell from my mother that she was from British Columbia. It is from these two pieces of information alone that I search. I have not thrown away all my roots yet and gone mobile—my only real chance—but I have not been completely idle, either. I do suppose that my hope still remains that the matter will be resolved by some wondrous miracle. In any case, what will be is for the best—this I know. I only hope that wherever my Lady may be, she is happy—and I wish this for her with all my heart.

A severely sprained ankle in the spring caused me a lot of grief and forced me to wash back a few classes in Nav School. Increasingly, my thoughts and diary entries focused on Valerie. In mid-June, I reached the 2,500-day mark since I last saw Valerie. On June 19th I wrote:

2500 days since I last saw Valerie. Perhaps one day the days will again number zero. I have lived and relived that day over and over again (in hundreds of different variations) in my mind ever since the count first went to one...but there does come a point where one has so little information to go upon that the trail is all but lost—and a miracle then becomes about the only hope of continuing such an adventure successfully. Such miracles do occur but must not be counted upon. I know I will see her again, somewhere—perhaps in that beautiful land I have dreamed of.

While I'm not a collector of material things, and I'm certainly not one to focus devotion towards such inanimate objects, I have occasionally sought out items that I think will remind me of the things I value. Much as an office building may post inspirational posters to keep their team members positively focused, I sometimes add items of inspiration to my environment. When my mind strays to places it need not go, a sword upon the wall or a moose upon the bookcase can bring me back. In July of 1989, while exploring in the old part of Sacramento, I stumbled upon a wonderful Lladro Don Quixote statue. What I remember most are the eyes. While kneeling and holding his lance, the great hero was gazing up at the heavens with an expression of true devotion. I was inspired. However, at $200, the statue was beyond my budget. I was used to having to temper my desires, pure though they might be, with the realities of my fiscal and professional well-being. After a long look, I had to walk away. However, with me, it's not always as easy as that. When I am inspired, common sense occasionally takes a back seat. I returned to the store several weeks later, intent on gazing upon the statue once more. However, I wasn't yet convinced that I should part with my money. Much to my distress, the statue was gone! I asked the store owner if they planned to restock this Lladro. They did not. When I inquired about ordering it, I was told it would take several months. There was no way it would make it in time for the magical month of August. The store owner was nice enough to call several other stores to inquire whether or not they carried it. In all cases, the response was no. I felt frustrated and disappointed. My monetary concerns had lost me an opportunity to purchase an inspirational artifact. I had only myself to blame. To this day, I remember that sinking feeling and the memory remained very fresh on numerous occasions where I stood staring at items in store windows.

Not one to admit defeat so swiftly, I drove to numerous malls in the area, looking for my statue. Again, I came away empty-handed. But, like during the Moose Hunts of old, I persisted on my quest. I returned home, drew my sword, and dove into the phone book. Luck would have it that I found a regional Lladro headquarters listed in the directory. I called ahead and they said they had the statue. I leaped into my car and was off in a flash. Perhaps it was no coincidence that several early War Years psych songs came on the radio as I was driving. Now, this was a Moose Hunt!

When I arrived at the store, my jaw nearly dropped. It was huge! The store encompassed several floors; and there were beautiful Lladro statues everywhere, including a quite enormous Don Quixote statue that was absolutely outside my budgetary range. Still, I was impressed. I searched and was unable to find my statue. Finally, I had to ask for assistance. They knew me from the phone call. I was told that the only version they had was the matte finish. This was a little bit of a disappointment since I really liked the glossy statue I had seen. However, I was unwilling to turn my back on this opportunity. The merchant visited one of the display cases and returned with a statue...but not my statue. It was another Don Quixote statuette. I explained that this wasn't the one I was looking for. The manager had to go back and look at their stock book. Good news! The store manager discovered that she did, indeed, have one (and only one) statue left, and it was the glossy finish statue that I wanted. I was thrilled! Best yet, the statue was officially named "The Quest." That seemed to be very appropriate. The fact that the statue was made in Spain added a little extra to its value and meaning. This time, I purchased the statue without any hesitation. As I drove back home, more special songs "coincidentally" played on the radio station I was listening to. It was a very special day and a very special Moose Hunt, or should I say "quest." I unboxed and set up the statue as I began my August battle on the anniversary of the day I first met Valerie, August 2nd.

On August 2, 1989, I began the "Great War of the Seven Year Quest." Besides unveiling my Don Quixote statue, I was also blessed with good fortune in that our navigator training flight profile for the night took us on the Polaris route, directly over Vancouver, B.C., Canada. As we flew over Vancouver, I said "I love you, Valerie" aloud. That was very special. Several other special events during the day inspired me and set the stage for a magnificent month to honor Valerie and the Cause. On August 5th, Don Quixote and I held vigil together throughout the night. Twenty-four hours without sleep, we both welcomed the sun and the dawning of a new day.

Don Quixote Statue

On the 12th, I dedicated the day to Moose Hunting in downtown Sacramento. My adventures took me to the library, a map store, and a bookstore. This inspirational outing was a paving stone on the road to Vancouver. I was intent on acquiring the necessary maps and guidebooks that might inform my greatest quest ever. As strong as my desire was, this story's ink was yet more likely to be found upon the pages of a fairy tale book than upon the sheets of a calendar. I knew the trip wasn't yet possible, but that did not dampen my enthusiasm. It remained a journey that I had to take. My diary recounts several notable "coincidences" occurring during my excursion into Sacramento. At the bookstore, I encountered a man talking about the Crusades while I was searching for guide books and books on knights and chivalry. At the library, I revisited the Vancouver phone directory. Still no Valerie. All in all, it was a wonderful day. I came home with several books and maps. The books and maps were important, but the day dedicated to Valerie was the real triumph. A diary entry from the following days sums up the passion within my heart:

> *Oh my dear Valerie, how my heart does yearn for you. So strong now are my thoughts of you that I feel imprisoned in that I cannot set forth this day in search of you. (...) Alas, perhaps in this life my Lady and I shall not again meet—but I know that one day, in one world or another, we shall again be together. This knowledge comforts me.*

On the 15th, I headed out for another short Moose Hunt to get some detailed city maps for Vancouver from the map store that had previously been closed when I visited. With city maps in hand, I now felt prepared for my great Moose Hunt. Of special note, as I departed the map store, I saw a purple balloon with purple streamers drifting by. As purple was Valerie's color, I just knew that this was a divine message. I was on the right path. My journey would have to wait a little while...but I was on the right path.

Summer gave way to autumn, and the cool breezes comforted my soul. Life in California was still somewhat lonely for me. I had an opportunity to visit my Great Aunt who was, in turn, visiting San Francisco with a friend. I also managed to get myself stranded in Hawaii when a severe ear infection prevented me from returning home with my aircraft on our oceanic "cross country" flight mission to Hickam Air Force Base. I gained a certain amount of fame for being the lieutenant who scored an all-expenses-paid vacation to Hawaii courtesy of the U.S. government. Considering all the pain and ill-effects of my ailment, I would have gladly traded the "vacation" for my health because palm trees and beaches aren't that much fun when you feel like a railroad spike has been driven through your ear.

In October, a massive 7.0 earthquake devastated nearby San Francisco. I was driving to pick up my new bicycle when I felt the ground shake, even though I was in Sacramento. Earthquake aside, it was great to have a bike again. The freedom I felt while riding my bicycle was the closest I was likely to come to riding a horse across the country. I clearly equated the two. I also began another battle, "The Battle of the Misty Mountains." This battle would be a very strong effort and would take me all the way into December.

During this time, my thoughts frequently drifted towards matters of destiny. From November 26, 1989:

Sure, I have my share of "what ifs"—we all do—but all in all, I am content with my past—it is all a part of me now. Besides—suppose I had told Valerie how much I love her—and suppose she had to coldly turn me away (not that she would have turned me away coldly, nice girl that she is)—then how would I be now? Without her inspiration over these many years, I dread to think of how my life might be now. Perhaps the same, perhaps someone else would have filled "the slot"— but I am inclined to think not. Even still, when I toy with the idea of trying to see her, I am very unsure. Almost no meeting could live up to my dreams and a poor meeting could jeopardize one of my greatest sources of inspiration—what a price. In the end, however, I know that destiny will guide my actions and whatever comes of it, comes with a purpose. I may not like it, at first, but just like that sour tasting medicine—the one your parents must force down your throat—in the end, it will surely be for the best.

After numerous classes, flights, and simulator missions, I took my final test at Nav School on December 15th and passed with a 97.5% to complete the long journey. Several days later, on December 19th, I finally earned my wings! It was a great day—the culmination of years of Academy training and flight training. All that remained between me and my first operational flying assignment was KC-135 Combat Crew Training School (CCTS). I felt ready for that challenge.

An inspirational trip home followed, and then it was back to business. I was getting stronger and stronger. I arrived at Castle Air Force Base, California on January 22, 1990. Training was busy, but I felt much more comfortable than I had in any previous flight training program. For the first time, I began to feel that my efforts were paying off and that my hard work would translate into success.

Specialized Undergraduate Navigator Training (SUNT)
photo, 1989

Flight training aside, I rolled into February feeling very strong; and on Valentine's Day, 1990, I got an extra boost. I watched an inspirational movie until bedtime; and when it was over, I thought

I'd flip through the channels just once prior to hitting the sack. Just as I flipped to MTV, the rarely seen music video for Steve Winwood's "Valerie" was starting up. I knew that this was no coincidence. This was a sign sent to me on Valentine's Day and I was oh so grateful and very inspired.

Ground training progressed to flight training at the Tanker School House, and I continued to perform well. The occasional visits to Monterey and Carmel helped to set my mind at ease. The sea always had a way of calming me and filling my soul with a peaceful feeling.

On April 25, 1990, I passed my final check ride, in spite of all kinds of bizarre changes, stormy weather, and other strange issues that I had never seen before. It went really well, and I had overcome the final hurdle to being an operational navigator in the Air Force. With my flight training finally complete on April 27th, I was on the road to Wichita, Kansas, and my first operational assignment. Mission complete!

Chapter Ten

PRELUDE TO A DREAM

I arrived at McConnell Air Force Base on the 29th of April, 1990, after two and a half days on the road from California. Almost immediately, I was entered into mission certification training. Nearly a month later, on May 25th, I received a message to call my former instructor at Castle Air Force Base; and he had some very good news to relay to me. I had earned Distinguished Graduate honors from the Combat Crew Training School as the #1 ranked graduate in my class. After the Academy and my pilot training experience, I had all but given up any hope that I would ever be number one at anything again. This was a wonderful surprise and a huge boost to my self-confidence.

Eventually, I began to settle into a routine. My time was divided between flying, completing ground training, and sitting Strategic Air Command Alert. With some stability finally returning to my life, the impossible adventures that I had resigned to the world of my dreams started to seem more attainable.

KC-135R refueling F-16 fighters

These dreams only grew stronger as August approached. When my parents visited in July and brought with them my box of "Secret Stuff" from home, I was quickly reliving memories inspired by all the inspirational things I had collected over the years—old diaries, an assortment of collectibles, and my Valerie folder. On August 2nd, I kicked off the month with an anniversary battle, "The Great Eighth Anniversary Battle: Search for the White Egret." The power was growing within. I was on Alert when I began the battle, so my initial vow was taken with a little plastic sword I had brought with me for the purpose. In my August 2nd diary entry, I explain the battle's name:

What I recall are several days—chilling, dark, and windy Autumn days—that I spent alone at the park, looking out across the ocean— my only company a white egret. So pure. It kept me company as I dreamed of Valerie across the ocean. And so great was my love—hours and hours that bird and I were there. One thing that made it particularly interesting is that, until that year, I had never before seen egrets at our park—only ducks and geese. And only two, total, were there—I could not help but feel it was some sign. I learned so much from the wind, the clouds, and the sea—my soul filled and I became what I am today. I hope that I never lose this "me." So, as I celebrate the eighth anniversary, I also seek out that inspiration and that pure belief—I seek out the white egret—for, in some way, I feel magically united with that bird and I've never believed that it was mere chance that brought us together. Though often this life is not conducive to chasing rainbows, I must keep faith in the world I know and love, my world, for it need not be part of 'theirs.'

After this, I finally revealed my big plans...but only to the protective pages of my diary. With our annual crew leave (10 days) scheduled for the end of August, I saw an opportunity for a grand quest...a Moose Hunt to top all Moose Hunts! I revealed my intent to travel to British Columbia. Although I was keenly aware that there was almost no chance of seeing Valerie, I knew it was a journey I must take. I naturally assumed she must have gotten married and changed her name since, in all my years of searching, I had never come across her name in any phone book. My diary entry seems to foretell some great saga as I emphasize that it would take some "Heaven-ordained" miracle to unite me with my Lady. I didn't feel that such a miracle was in the cards even though my heart was telling me never to give up hoping or lose faith. In my diary, I also consider that, should I ever find her again, I would likely lose my mind and my voice and, just like in Spain, be unable to express what was boiling over in my heart. Even amidst my doubts, I considered this adventure to be the most holy of all my pilgrimages. I really didn't know what to expect, but I had a strong feeling that this Moose Hunt would be of great value to my soul.

As I began the first stages of planning for a trip to another country, I was secretly hoping for a magical journey to another realm altogether. I wanted to cross the bridge; I wanted to return to my world.

But, like in any good saga, the winds of fate cast a dark cloud of uncertainty over my planned adventure. On August 2, 1990, Iraq invaded Kuwait; and the United States was in the fight. I was told to pack my bags and prepare to deploy. My leave and my great adventure seemed to be in serious jeopardy. I was very interested in getting into the fight, but the timing of this whole mess seemed very unfortunate. As increased information came to us about the high risk to our deployed forces, I knew I had to be part of this—it's what my whole Air Force journey had been about. However, I truly hoped that, before my possible death in combat, I might have the opportunity to go on one final great adventure to the sacred lands from whence my lady came.

At work, our schedule became completely unpredictable as crews were told to ready themselves to deploy and the Alert schedule was completely rearranged. I stood to lose quite a bit of money if my trip to Canada was canceled, but I also didn't want to miss out on any of the wartime action. I committed that, should my leave be canceled, I would never give up trying to get up to Vancouver. The signs continued to come. August 12th, for example, was Steve Winwood day on the VH1 music television station and videos for "Valerie," "Paper Sun," and "Mr. Fantasy" inspired me, along with some concert scenes with "Can't Find My Way Home" and other Winwood greats. Many of these songs formed the soundtrack of my magical awakening in the months following my return from Spain. I knew the timing could not be coincidental.

When they come alone, signs can often be overlooked. As August progressed, it became evidently clear that there was real magic in the air. On August 16th, as I once again assumed Alert duty, I noticed a *National Geographic* magazine lying on top of my dresser as I entered my room. On the cover of the magazine was a white egret, just like the ones I saw back at Saddle Rock Park—the one I named my current battle after. Another sign! In my diary I wrote:

> *Things are happening—magic is slowly misting the air, once more. I see wisps and traces here and there and I know that we may do more than just live and then die.*

With many of our McConnell tankers and crews heading overseas, it was certainly a strange and exciting time. We had heard rumors, later confirmed by a Strategic Air Command headquarters briefing, that simulation calculations indicated we would lose somewhere between twenty and thirty percent of all the KC-135s in the first two nights of a war with Iraq. I knew I had to be part of this effort. I also knew that I had one last thing I needed to do before I died—and that was travel to Vancouver on my holy quest.

Despite all my planning and hoping, the chance that my leave would go through seemed increasingly unlikely, with everything going on.

On August 28th, I twisted my ankle very badly playing basketball. After three previous sprained ankles, you think I would have learned my lesson. For better or worse, I loved sports too much to quit. Limping about, I found my foot was solid enough to walk on; but I was very aware of how close I came to another catastrophe. On the 29th, a day prior to coming off my current Alert tour, I was still unsure whether my leave would survive. It would.

Chapter Eleven

MIRACLES

After coming off Alert, on the morning of August 30th, I felt a strange sense of freedom. I visited the mall to pick up a ceramic lighthouse I had ordered, and then I purchased a copy of the movie *Camelot* from another store in the mall. With my great adventure just hours away, I wanted to make sure that I appropriately set the stage for the adventure. I also drew my sword back at Eagle Rock Apartments and readied myself. Hopping in my blue and silver Chevrolet S-10 Blazer, I left my apartment at 3:20 pm. Almost immediately, "things" started to happen. Not long after turning on my car radio, the song "Ramble On" came on. I was amazed! This, more than any song, captured who I was and the spirit of my eight-year quest. Shortly thereafter, another classic song from my early War Years came on the radio. This time, it was "I'm Free" by the Who. I felt the power surging into my heart. There was no doubt—magic was in the air and I wasn't just driving to the airport; I had "crossed the bridge" and was driving back into my world!

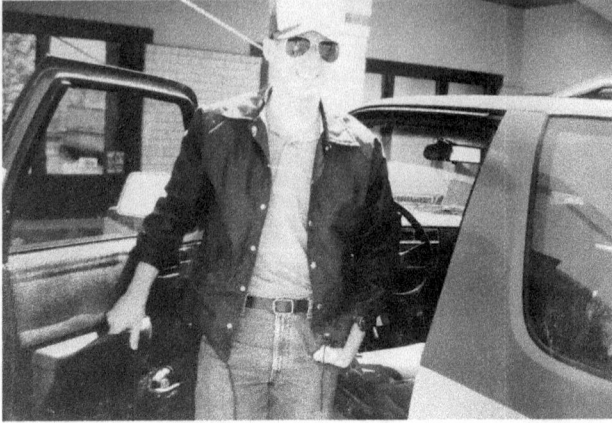

"Road ready," just prior to my trip to Vancouver

I boarded my Continental Airlines DC-9 at a little after 5:00 pm, and we were airborne seventeen minutes later. My travel day would take me through Denver, Colorado, and Spokane, Washington. The final leg of my air travel was the short hop up to Vancouver, B.C. It was raining fairly heavily in Vancouver when we touched down. I rented a black Ford Tempo and, with maps in hand, began trying to find my hotel. The heavy rain must have disoriented me a little bit because it took over an hour to get to my hotel. I only later discovered that my lodging, the Executive Inn Hotel, was only a short twenty-minute drive from the airport. How typical for a navigator to get lost on the roads of Vancouver. At 10:46 pm (past midnight back in Wichita, Kansas), I finally checked into room 205 and logged my travel complete. I was exhausted, but my spirit was filling quickly as dreams were transitioning into reality.

International Arrivals, Vancouver International Airport

I woke up at 8:50 am and cleaned up. Before beginning my day's business with a planned first stop at a local bank to exchange my money, I had a crazy notion. I thought that I might check the drawers of my nightstand to see if there was a current Vancouver phone book present. Luck would have it that there was—and it was nearly brand new! I was looking at the July 1, 1990, edition! I had very recently looked at the 1989 edition of the Vancouver phone book and, as usual, came up empty-handed. So, I had absolutely no expectation of finding anything. I wasn't even sure I should look...but I did. From my diary:

This morning, my heart all but stopped when I stumbled upon a V. Dudoward in the phone book. Now, who knows what that "V" stands for. It could be some guy or, even if it was for "Valerie," perhaps it would not be the right one. But there's a one in a million chance—perhaps even better. Thus, my heart has been trembling in a wild, yet wonderful, way today. So—what's the problem? Well, the same problem as in 1982, with a few added variables.

I've spent 8 years dreaming, my savings to finance, and my leave to launch this great adventure—yet I'm still scared. To act would truly be not 100% normal, yet I believe my decision to go through with this trip mostly answered this. But—if the V. Dudoward listed is not my Lady, wouldn't it make this trip that much more exciting to put the matter off—already I've had non-stop wonderful daydreams and a wonderful walk by the sea just imagining the possibilities [the walk by the sea refers to my 2:45 pm fifty-minute walk along the beach at Jericho Park]. But also—suppose I did wish to try to arrange a meeting, and it was her—I would want to give her enough warning to better the chances of arranging a good time. And, if I should discover that it is not her, then am I really any worse than before—no, not really. And, it would allow me some more days to research in town and free me up for touring (though touring was not the primary objective of this mission). These questions and others race through my mind. What to do? What to do? And there I sat in the lobby of our hotel in Torremolinos—waiting and wondering if "she" was to pass by, would I truly find the courage to speak with her. What would I say?

When does one cross the line between reality and fantasy? Does such a line even exist? Perhaps such things are best left to dreams.

Jericho Park, first full day in Vancouver (August 31, 1990)

My mind was flooded with scenarios, and I knew the trip to Jericho Park would help me sort it all out. I paced up and down the beach, much as I had paced back and forth within my hotel room after making the discovery. The day was cool and cloudy and ripe for wandering thoughts. Numerous logs were positioned along the shore; and occasionally, I would sit upon one, stare out across the water, and ponder. I got back to my hotel at 4:23 pm and my stomach tightened as I drew closer to resolving my dilemma. In all truth, I knew there could be only one resolution—I just needed the courage to pursue it.

At 7:05 pm, I picked up the phone receiver and dialed the number. It was not Valerie who answered, but another woman. I inquired about the "Valerie" at this address and asked if she had ever mentioned taking a trip to Spain in 1982. The woman responded that Valerie was asleep at present and, apparently, quite ill. She mentioned Valerie had been sick for quite some time. I was devastated to hear this news! The woman did confirm, however, that Valerie had spoken of an American Express trip to Spain in her past. I had found my Lady! I left my number, and the woman on the phone assured me that she would pass the information on to Valerie and that she would probably attempt to call me back. We exchanged farewells and the receiver went back upon the phone. From my diary entry, moments after the call:

Now I feel the knight come alive within my soul—for too long I have been idle and concerned with self, assuming my Lady (God Bless Her!) was well and happy and better off without me. Have I been such a fool?! As surely as my Lady has saved me from sadness unmatched, I must never give up wishing her well—not any day, not any minute— never! For if I have power in this arm of mine, or within my soul— then let it, please God, be used to protect the innocent and true and uphold the Right. Let me protect her who saved me—let me save my Lady Valerie for she is so very dear to me. I only pity that it has taken me so long to realize this.

I know that miracles do happen—I have seen many—and the fact that the first time I should find my Lady is the one time I sally forth upon this Great Quest (and in the July 1, 1990, phonebook edition) is more than proof enough.

Have I been such a poor friend that all along I have looked to Valerie for help when, perhaps, I should have made greater efforts to give her some of my own? Such thoughts run through my mind and trouble me for, surely, I can be a better friend than I have been. My Lady needs my help and I shall not fail her! For Valerie is and forever shall be my Lady. Please forgive me if I have been weak—for I have wavered over the years. But, I have never fallen and I never shall! I must keep the faith, always!

Once upon a bus, a shy young man felt in his heart the desire to give his jacket to a sick Lady who was chilled by the air conditioning on a bus [filled with tourists who demanded it from the heat]. But this shy lad didn't have the courage to offer it. Let not this happen again. Offer your jacket to your Lady for it is your armor and protects you— let it protect her who you love. There are many jackets to be offered in this world yet too few pass hands. Remember from your mistakes, lad, and the lessons taught you shall not have been in vain.

Just a week before, I thought that I might simply head across the border and dream a few nice dreams, tour a little bit, and return. My trip had just become something entirely new. I had truly entered into my world and the opportunity for a holy quest was put before me. But, I had to be brave and I had to be true. With a growing headache and a mind racing with thoughts, I went out for a sub sandwich for dinner and was in bed by 10:00 pm (though certainly not able to fall asleep). What a way to spend the final day of the "magical month of August!"

The next day, September 1st, I awoke with a heart filled with hope and filled with concern for my lady. During the night, I had had a magnificent, yet very cryptic, Valerie dream. I had to take note. There was magic about, to be sure. I had planned to end my August battle on the last day of the month; but with so much magic in the air, it seemed only appropriate to continue my anniversary battle for a while longer. My soul was so filled with spirit that I knew this had to be. Like the days before, the climate perfectly suited me—sixty-five degrees Fahrenheit, overcast skies, and a cool breeze. It was perfect—absolutely perfect. I felt the need to wander, yet I also felt tied to a telephone that I was unsure would ever ring. Had Valerie received the message? If she had, did she have any idea who this David Lange guy was, and would she be inclined to return the call, if not? Still, I was concerned about her health. Sick since winter; that's what her friend had told me. That's a very long time to be ill, and my mind ran through numerous terrible diseases and conditions that might cause such a long-spanning illness. I was very worried.

Dutifully, I established a vigil aside my phone...and I wondered. Finally, at 11:20 am, I went to get lunch at the hotel's restaurant and returned as quickly as I could. No messages. After much debate, I decided that it would be unwise to spend my entire trip waiting by the phone. That's not the way of the knight. I would venture forth and God would ensure that things worked out as they were meant to be. I began considering my contingency plan—what would I do should a meeting never materialize? Perhaps a letter? I would give the matter some more thought. A little after 1:00 pm, I ventured forth to Queen Elizabeth Park and, later, to the Maritime Museum. The park was beautiful—brightly blooming flowers created a lovely mosaic. The museum was interesting but not very substantial. I was in and out within an hour and a half.

Upon returning to my hotel, I ran out to grab a sandwich at Mr. Submarine, just down the road, and brought it back to my room. Still no messages. I ate dinner in the room, watched television, and daydreamed...a lot. Eventually, I drifted off to sleep.

I slept in late the next morning. With my mind racing, falling asleep was no easy task. I eventually pulled myself out of bed at 10:16 am, and I knew I needed to take action. Knights must be brave. I couldn't spend another half day wandering around my room waiting for the phone to ring. I nervously paced back and forth, until I had nearly worn out the carpet. I was desperately trying to work up the courage to call Valerie's number. At 11:30 am, I was finally able to bring myself to dial the number, after half a dozen glasses of water, numerous trips to the bathroom, and countless yards of pacing. Valerie answered! Her voice was beautiful. The dulcet tones, the gentleness, and the warmth were just as I remembered. It had been eight years since I had last heard Valerie speak, but everything about her voice was immediately recognizable. I was thrilled beyond description. We talked for over fifteen minutes on all manner of things. Most importantly, I thanked her for helping to change my life for the better. I was still unsure if we'd ever meet in person, so it was absolutely critical for me that I use this opportunity to personally thank her. It felt wonderful to finally let her know. I felt like a weight had lifted off of me, and I felt at peace. Better still, we set up a lunch date for Wednesday, the 5th of September. She passed me her work phone; the plan being that I would call her at work and then we would finalize the details for our rendezvous.

In the course of our discussion, she mentioned that she had drifted around quite a bit between various places in British Columbia and even Mexico. She said that she had only just recently returned to Vancouver. I knew that the timing of my visit had to be divinely driven. It was a true miracle! In the short duration of our phone conversation, hearing her sweet and kind voice, I knew that she was completely real—I had not created an angel out of thin air. She was the real thing—a wonderful and caring person—my Lady Valerie. Valerie also told me how she was currently doing social work with First Nations people. In Canada, the name is used to refer to Canada's indigenous population, just as we refer to this population as Native Americans within the United States. My faith was reaffirmed—Valerie was truly one of the beautiful people in this world. I didn't know at the time, but Valerie, herself, was a proud Tsimshian woman.

I was so excited about the phone call that I completely ignored meal times. I was out the door at half-past noon for Stanley Park and what would be a wonderful day of sightseeing. My first stop was at the aquarium. The aquarium was clean and beautiful; and the zoo park, while not substantial, was also very enjoyable. Stanley Park, itself, was a wonderful place to relax and think. The wooded areas brought to mind enchanted forests from the story-books. One of the things I remember best from my day at the park was a wonderful old-fashioned puppet show taking place in the middle of an open field. A little puppet theater was set up; and children gathered all around, laughing and clapping at the antics of the characters. It was a lovely production, and I enjoyed not only the show but everything about the scene. Elsewhere in the park, artists worked diligently at their easels, translating their visions into colorful symphonies on canvas. It was a picturesque scene of tranquility and peace. I remember the day fondly as one of the happiest and most peaceful days of my life. Everything about the day was perfect. The day was a lovely gift.

I eventually left the park and made my way back to my hotel room where I ordered a pizza. It was my first meal of the day. Positive energy, alone, seemed to have sustained me throughout the day's activities. September 2nd was one of my favorite days in Vancouver. I have since returned to Stanley Park on many occasions, but it never seemed to hold quite the same magic as it did on that day. One thing is always guaranteed—every visit brings with it a flood of memories—and my heart fills with happiness. I finished up my diary entry and called it a day, at twenty past eleven.

September 3rd was another day set aside for tourism. I slept in rather late, again, and departed my room after 10:00 am en route to Lighthouse Park. I've always been very fond of lighthouses, and I was looking forward to seeing one in person. I had visited a light-house in Maine with my family when I was a very young child, but the images had long since faded from my mind. As you may imagine, I was very excited when the lighthouse finally came into view. It was very impressive. However, I was even more impressed by the beauty of the trees in the park—they seemed very old and very majestic. Wandering along the various walking paths evoked images of enchanted forests from the old fairy tales. It certainly felt very magical. I felt very much at peace. Vancouver is a truly beautiful place—absolutely breathtaking!

Lighthouse Park (September 3, 1990)

My next stop for the day was the famous Capilano Suspension Bridge. At 450 feet long, and suspended 230 feet above the valley floor, in 1990 the bridge laid claim to being the world's longest suspension bridge. I really enjoyed traveling back and forth across the chasm. Once again, the scenery was spectacular. I have to admit that I was amused watching several bridge-goers clutch desperately to the side ropes on the bridge, clearly frozen in absolute terror. For my part, I equated the swaying bridge with the peaceful motion of a ship at sea. Naturally, it wasn't quite the same —the swaying wooden planks of the bridge could simulate the roll but not the pitch of an ocean-going vessel. At just after 2:00 pm, I grabbed a late lunch at the bridge snack bar and then began the hour-long drive back to my hotel room. Once again, I stopped for a sub sandwich just down the road from the hotel and brought it back for dinner, reserving the rest of the evening for daydreaming and reflection. I closed out my diary entry for the day with these words:

> *Sort of weird—dreaming for 8 years of seeing Valerie again—in a lunch, what can one say—8 years of thought and planning could never prepare one for such a moment—so I think I will do as I have thought I might—just be me—no speeches, no preaching, no eloquent praises—just me and my friend and what I hope will be a pleasant lunch. Whatever I might say could never express my feelings so it is better I do not try. I have said my thanks—and this came from the heart—all else now is just icing on what was already a wonderful and very magical cake. Valerie is my lady—but let me not forget that she is my friend and one and the same with the beautiful girl from Canada who first caught my eye on that second day of August, 1982—Valerie.*

September 4th was another perfectly beautiful day in Vancouver. I had nearly no objectives for the day beyond gassing up my rental vehicle and mentally preparing myself for the projected meeting the next day with my lady.

Capilano Suspension Bridge (September 3, 1990)

I took lunch at the hotel restaurant at half past noon and then left the hotel for gas. I decided, on the way, that I would also visit the incredible Metrotown Mall. I did not spend very much time there, but I was there long enough to be pulled in by an amazing painting of a moose at the Nature's Window Art Gallery. I couldn't take my eyes off of the print—it seemed to be drawing me in, speaking to me in a way that only the heart can comprehend. For all its inspirational value, at $800 (and another $110 for shipment to the U.S.), the price tag was frustratingly beyond my financial means. I had spent a significant portion of my savings on the trip; and as a young Air Force lieutenant, I had long since learned to budget my limited financial resources. I wasn't ready to drop that kind of money just yet. Steve Winwood's "Back in the High Life" played while I was at the mall—and I was, indeed, back in the high life. When I returned to my hotel room, I purchased a small moose plaque at the hotel gift store—perhaps my way of compensating for letting the $800 painting slip away. I closed my diary again with some reflections to typify the thoughts swirling around in my brain:

> Forgive me if I have not spoken much as to what is to occur tomorrow —it is no easy topic to address for it is like critiquing a dream. What comes to pass will be as destiny would have it. I am trying to downplay the significance in my mind so that I don't psych myself out. I hope that I can have a pleasant lunch with a friend and if I stop to think that I am about to see my Lady—who has inspired me and who I have believed in these many years—then I shall surely have some difficulty dealing with the moment in a normal, down to earth fashion. I should remember that I knew and loved Valerie as a person long before I had idolized her as my Lady. Yet, I do not wish to, in any way, lessen in my mind my level of respect/belief/reverence/etc. for her—for I need her as my Lady (which she is and will always be) as I need her as my friend. Also, I must remember—this is my dream, and my world—it may not necessarily be hers, too. Thus, I must show some

tact in my actions. Valerie Dudoward is a wonderful human being and I wish not to do anything to confuse her or give her stress. Nay, I wish only to cheer her and, perhaps, if I might, inspire her as well. But, I could never inspire her as she inspired me. So, perhaps, David, it is best not to put too much thought into the matter—just do as seems Right and, perhaps, when you must once again bid a sad farewell to this great lady (assuming lunch goes through as planned)—then you may sit back and look at what great miracles have taken place these past several days and you shall know that this world is Good and you shall have Faith in all you believe for the lessons you learned 8 years ago live—inspired by a Great Lady—Dear, Sweet, Valerie."

The 5th of September finally came; but unfortunately, the day did not unfold as I would have hoped. My entire morning was spent with butterflies zipping about in my stomach in anticipation of the call to Valerie's workplace, as we had prearranged, to resolve the final plan for our lunch date. And there was, of course, some pretty major nervousness associated with the prospect of actually seeing Valerie again.

After a late start to my day, I went out for some air and to try to de-stress a little bit. At the appointed time, 1:00 pm, I called Valerie's office only to be informed that she was home, ill. My mind filled with countless thoughts and scenarios. First, and foremost, I was concerned about Valerie and her health. I already knew she had a track record of health issues throughout the year. Was this yet another bout of whatever ailment was assailing her? I was worried. Amidst these more noble thoughts, I began to wonder if our meeting was simply not destined to be. I called her apartment several times throughout the day, but all I got was an answering machine. As I considered that she might be resting, it did not strike me as odd that no one was picking up the phone. I hoped my calls were not disturbing her. I can't deny there was a part of me that thought, perhaps, she might have no desire to meet up with a veritable stranger—someone she hadn't seen in over eight years and might not even remember. While plausible, my heart wasn't buying that explanation. I firmly believed that Valerie would have been honest with me if this was the case. But, suppose she didn't want to hurt me? My mind worked its way through multiple scenarios. I left a message on Valerie's answering machine wishing her well. In my diary entry for the day, I contemplated the meaning of it all. Ultimately, I resolved, most unambiguously, that my faith in Valerie was well-founded. I trusted her. I loved her. Ultimately, I contented myself with the fact that, regardless of whether the in-person meeting ever happened, the journey had already surpassed all my expectations. I reflected on how I finally found the opportunity that I had been dreaming of for so many years—a chance to say "thank you, Valerie." As I quickly resolved any internal confusion, I still had to ponder how my remaining days in Vancouver would play out. I did not want to spend my remaining days in Vancouver staring at my hotel room phone. I thought I might, perhaps, sign up for some tours. I was still worried that any extended absence might result in a missed phone call. Such a call would truly be a blessed event. Missing such a call would be a sure-fire recipe for heartbreak. I weighed my options carefully.

With the day free for thinking and the possibility of a meeting with my lady now even more questionable, I set out to compose a letter that I might deliver to her or mail to her; one that set forth, in great detail, all that I felt she should know—everything. Everything about a hopeless, lost, youth, and the beautiful person who saved him from himself. Everything about a loyal knight and the lady he sought to honor through deeds and a true heart. Everything. It was the full and complete thank you that I knew I could never deliver verbally. The lengthy letter was truly a labor of love.

That night I ate dinner at the hotel, my only meal for the day, and went to bed at 10:00 pm. My all-too-brief morning walk had been my only escape from the confines of my hotel room. But the day was not a loss—it was filled with thoughts and dreams of Valerie and with the creation of a heartfelt letter to my lady.

The 6th, as it turns out, was a much brighter and hope-filled day. Any doubts and woe from the previous day were more than eradicated after I called Valerie at work and she promptly returned my phone call with an enthusiastic and fully fleshed out plan for our rendezvous. We set a firm date for September 7th and picked the time and place for the meeting. There would be no further phone calls for coordination—we would meet at 1:30 pm on the 7th at the Shenanigan's lounge pub on Robson Street. Although my heart was still proceeding cautiously, I was definitely back in a place of inner peace after Valerie's gentle and kind words. She informed me that she had recently been suffering from some very bad allergy issues which, when combined with some other goings-on in her life, had made things very difficult for her. Valerie told me that she was really looking forward to seeing me again. Her words made my heart soar. I was so afraid that she might consent to the meeting out of pity or just to be kind. To hear that she was so enthusiastic about our get together made a tremendous positive impact on my psyche. It was a wonderful phone call.

Having just spoken to my lady, and now having the remainder of the day free to venture forth without fear of missing a call, I knew there was one mission that needed to be accomplished and that today was the day to do it. I left the hotel at noon and headed back to the Metrotown Mall. After a quick lunch featuring some gourmet hot dogs at the Mall, I returned to the Nature's Window Art Gallery and re-engaged on the cost of the moose painting that I had been so captivated by. The piece was a limited-edition print by the artist Robert Bateman called "The Challenge: Bull Moose." While the multi-matted presentation at the shop was incredibly beautiful, I thought I could shave a few hundred dollars off the incredibly high price if I opted for a simpler framing option. I was right. With two hundred knocked off the price, the print re-entered into the realm of the financially feasible; and I committed to buying it and having it shipped back to the United States. It was a huge investment; but to this very day, I have never regretted the purchase. A magically powerful depiction of this very special animal purchased on the same day that I had a warm conversation with Valerie—how could I pass it up? The print would forever remind me of the special and very magical pilgrimage to Vancouver. And, just to add an exclamation point onto the day, I also visited a bookstore at the mall and purchased copies of Homer's *Iliad* and *The Odyssey*. I was living my own saga.

Framed moose painting purchased in Vancouver

I returned to my hotel room at half-past three and had dinner at the hotel's restaurant which now considered me a regular. After dinner, I took a very nice walk to get some fresh air and sort through all the many thoughts and emotions coursing through my mind. I was so mentally preoccupied that I neglected to even record a bedtime for the day. I do know I had a very difficult time actually trying to get to sleep, so any recorded bedtime would be irrelevant. The events planned for the next day seemed completely impossible—I had never been so close, in all my life, to actually realizing a dream.

September 7, 1990. My diary entry begins, appropriately:

Mark this Day & Remember it for all time! 'Twas in the year of our Lord, One Thousand, Nine-hundred and Ninety, on the 7th day of September, that a knight, after having quested for eight long years— did once again find and greet his Lady—and look into her eyes and know that life and this world were Good!

I awoke fairly early but stayed in bed, thinking and daydreaming, until nearly 10:00 am. I didn't really know what else to do. I had one goal for the day—one, and only one, sacred task. As the clock steadily ticked, marking the passage of time, I found myself getting more and more nervous. I carefully picked out my clothes —I would wear my best. For me, this meant my favorite green polo shirt and a nice pair of blue jeans. I would never depart on such a journey without my armor, so I wore my blue windbreaker and baseball cap as I departed my hotel room at noon. I had already paid multiple visits to the bathroom that morning. My nervous stomach was getting the better of me. I also drank an abundance of water to lubricate my drying throat. Although our meeting wasn't planned until 1:30 pm, I left with all kinds of extra time available to account for any and all manner of mischance. At 1:06

pm, I arrived at the pay parking lot at Thurlow and Alberni. After parking my rental car, I proceeded to the Blue Horizon Hotel where I began my timing orbits (to borrow an aviation term), anxiously pacing about, back and forth, in front of the hotel associated with the Shenanigan's lounge. I was so over-hydrated from all the nervous drinking that I had to make at least two visits to the restroom at the hotel. I was a bundle of nerves. I tried my best to hold it all together.

1:30 pm came and passed. I hoped that Valerie had not gotten sick again and canceled out. In the end, despite all my nervousness, I have to imagine that Valerie must have been somewhat anxious, too, at the prospect of meeting up with someone so obscure from her past. If she was, she never let it show.

At 1:45 pm, Valerie arrived and I recognized her immediately. She looked a little bit older but was still very much the Valerie I had remembered—so very vibrant and glowing. We hit it off right away and talked about countless things. My face was sore from smiling by the time we were done. Through nearly continuous smiles, we both pretty much laughed our way through the two hours we spent together. While we had originally intended to order lunch, neither of us ever did. Valerie did order a glass of wine and I stuck with water...but that was it. I'd tell a story, then Valerie would, and so on. I won't run down the many things we discussed—some topics were more personal than others—but it was truly wonderful. I remember discussing my horrible experience with water survival training; and she confided that she was a little afraid of the water, too. She told how someone had pushed her in a pool at a party when she was young and couldn't swim and that she nearly drowned and, ever since, had a lingering fear of drowning. Strangely enough, we both had a true love for the sea (so long as we weren't below the waves). As we talked about our love of being near the ocean, Valerie got off on a wonderful tangent about how the sea produced positive ions and that these were associated with health and a positive attitude. I still smile when I think of this discussion. It was a little "New-Agey" but I loved the logic behind the conclusions—I was spellbound. In later years, I almost purchased a home air purifier to clean the air in my home. When I read that it worked by cranking out lots of negative ions to attract the dust, I immediately thought of Valerie's warning about negative ions and dropped all thoughts of getting the device. In later years, I came across a number of negative reviews on that contraption. It seemed like I owed Valerie a debt of gratitude, yet again.

Our conversation did turn serious for a while as Valerie talked about some of the difficulties she was experiencing and how it was a challenging time in her life. She also mentioned that her father had only recently passed away and how the loss was a source of lingering sorrow. I felt very moved and wished to find some way, any way, that maybe I could help her.

We then both discussed what we had done since 1982—it was wonderful to catch up. I was so impressed by the work that Valerie was doing to help urban First Nations people and wished that my brother could be there to hear all about it. He'd fall in love, too. Valerie was never boastful and never spoke about the many great things she'd done in life. I did not learn about those until many years later. For Valerie, I think her personal greatest accomplishments were marked by the little things she did to help others each and every day. Our whole conversation was wonderfully relaxed and beautiful—it was very much like I was talking to a friend of many years. I felt completely at peace when I was with Valerie. In my diary, I note that I saw countless similarities between us and how things she said were so very much like things I might have said.

During our conversation, I made sure to thank her again for

the great impact she had on my life. Beyond this, I tried to steer clear of the really heavy stuff. After nearly two hours, at 3:36 pm, we finally decided it was time to part. I could have easily spent the day there with Valerie. She took out a little yellow sticky pad note and wrote down her address and phone numbers for me and told me that she would like to stay in touch and that she liked writing. I was thrilled! From my jacket, hung over the back of my chair, I pulled out the envelope with the very, very, long letter I had written a few days before, when I thought we might never meet. It was a total and complete heart-pouring-out of everything Valerie had meant to me and how she had truly changed my life for the better. I left little, if anything, out. I was unsure whether I would actually give it to her or not but, as we prepared to part, I realized that I needed to. She needed to know that she had changed my life and that I would be forever grateful. She needed to know that she had but to contact me and I would come to her aid in any capacity I could manage. I wanted to be her friend. I was her friend. The envelope containing the letter was simply labeled "Valerie." This was the REAL "THANK YOU" that I had been dreaming of sharing with Valerie for eight years. 2,941 days after I had last seen Valerie, at the Barajas Airport in Madrid, I finally got to do it right. As we got up and prepared to leave, I pulled my blue windbreaker off the back of my chair and snapped it up and then put on my blue baseball cap. Although Valerie had been smiling throughout our wonderful "lunch" together, an extra special and very beautiful smile stretched across her face when she saw me in the jacket and baseball cap—her eyes seemed to sparkle. She looked me in the eyes, with a beautiful and caring expression, and said simply "I remember now!" I think she finally saw, in this twenty-four-year-old young man, the young fifteen-year-old boy who had been so taken with her on the trip to Spain. It was a very, very, special moment. Not much more was said. She just stood there smiling at me and I was smiling back—it felt so very warm and special. That memory is one of the most beautiful ones I preserve within my mind. I pray it never fades. We walked out together and said our final farewells in front of Shenanigan's. She was heading right and I was heading left. It was very hard for me to leave, but I knew she had to get back to work; and two hours with an angel was much more than many people are ever blessed with. It would not be right for me to be greedy. After saying goodbye, properly, I turned and started walking back towards the lot where I had parked my vehicle. What happened next beautifully encapsulated Valerie's special and caring nature. I was probably a good ten paces down the sidewalk when I turned around to look back at Valerie—I wanted one last look. I expected to see her walking away. She was not. Valerie was still standing there, watching me. It was as if she wanted to be there for me, just in case I had even one more thing to say or if there was anything else I needed. An incredibly warm feeling came over me. It was indescribable. Just like during that one special dinner in Spain, there we were, the only two people on the face of the earth, gazing upon one another with warmth and caring hearts. I will always remember that moment. I knew I had said what needed to be said, and I was keenly aware that the blessings of the day were greater than anything I could have ever imagined. I was incredibly grateful. I knew it was time for me to take my leave. This was the very last time I ever saw Valerie. I don't know that any other final vision could have been more appropriate. It is a beautiful and special way to remember my Lady Valerie. Just as I remember her beautiful beaming face from Spain, I too shall never forget the feeling of being cared about as we parted for that last time. God bless Valerie!

Shenanigans

I returned to my car and was back at the hotel at 4:30 pm. My mind was still in an ethereal dreamy state, so my first order of business was to go for a walk to continue processing the events of the day. I remember very few times in my life where my heart was so at peace. I had dinner at the hotel that night and, when I returned to my room to settle in for the evening, I cannot say I was surprised when a nature show about moose was on the television. How appropriate! I watched the show in its entirety. I laid awake in bed for many hours before finally drifting, happily, off to sleep. It was a magical day.

My diary entry for the day goes on for quite a while, as you might imagine. One short paragraph, worth repeating, described my feelings:

And now—to return with Autumn pending—surely things are in a good way. Perhaps I shall be sent to Saudi Arabia and perhaps I will

see combat—perhaps I shall not return. But, with what has happened,
and after the miracles of late, I would not feel cheated nor that my life
was cut short. And, I know that whatever happens—a better world
awaits—and one in which I may perhaps finally be that which I do so
long to be—A Knight.

In the days that followed, I would be deployed out to the war
zone. But, my heart was still so very much at peace that I was
never afraid of death—that's how significant the events of the trip
to Vancouver and my completion of an eight-year quest had been.
Now that I had finally found Lady Valerie and thanked her properly, I felt my life was fulfilled.

There were yet a few days left on my trip to Vancouver. The
adventure had not yet run its course. No day would, or could,
match the day I had just lived. While my time in Spain was
magical and will live forever as some of my most treasured memories, there was something extra special about September 7, 1990—
something that never happened in Spain. For the first time, I had
Valerie all to myself and we were talking as friends. I cannot say it
enough—this was a blessing greater than anything I could have
ever hoped for and probably much greater than anything I
deserved. I am forever grateful for this!

During the course of our conversations that day, Valerie had
mentioned that she would like for me to meet her boyfriend and
that maybe we could all do something together. I was not sure
whether this was a legitimate desire of hers or whether it was
simply her nice way of telling me that she was seeing someone. I
told her that I would, of course, be interested in that and that I
would gladly be part of such an outing, should she desire to
arrange one. I really did not expect to hear back from her...but that
was okay. She had given me two amazing hours of her time and
proved, yet again, that she was an incredibly special and beautiful

person. No greater gift than this was possible. I made very loose and adaptable plans for my remaining few days in Vancouver.

The next day, I started late and had lunch in the hotel. I then went to visit Science World and the old Expo '86 Fairgrounds. Science World was very interesting. The fairgrounds were haunting. Memories of the shoulder-to-shoulder crowds from my visit back in 1986 came flooding back to me; but on this day, it was completely vacant. There's a song by a group called Renaissance that I still associate with this re-visit. It's called "Trip to the Fair" and the chorus goes: "I took a trip down to look at the fair, when I arrived I found nobody there, it seems I was all alone, must be that they've all gone home." My mind was adrift in memories. It was not a sad reflection, but it was powerful. Outside the museum, I shared the empty spaces with the seagulls—they were all the company I needed. After the visit, I returned to my hotel and ordered a pizza. While my agenda was light now, my mind was so filled with thoughts that I didn't really need a lot of activity to fill the hours of my day.

On September 9th, I returned to Jericho Park where I spent my first day thinking and dreaming of maybe getting to see Valerie again. It seemed very appropriate to return, on my last full day in Vancouver, for some more deep thought by the shore. I remembered a boy, standing at the fence line of Saddle Rock Park, looking West-Northwest towards British Columbia and towards my Lady. As a kind of special homage to this great quest, and the eight years of dreaming leading up to it, I turned East-Southeast and looked back towards where a younger me stood dreamily hoping that one day I might again find my Lady Valerie. It was a special moment.

Continuing my day within my hotel room, I took time, after dinner, to write some more in my diary. Unlike during our trip to

Spain, I actually had a diary and made sure I took time each night to recount some of my feelings following each day in Vancouver.

September 10th was my last day in Vancouver. I had an afternoon flight scheduled back to Wichita, Kansas. My concerns over the heartfelt, tell-all, letter that I had given to Valerie all faded at 8:32 am when I received the most pleasant wake-up call of my life. It was Valerie! She wanted to speak to me again before I left Vancouver. It was a very warm phone conversation. She had read my letter and wanted to thank me. She thanked me not only for the letter, and the kind words within, but also for having the courage to follow through on my quest and meet with her. She ended by wishing me well and stating again that she wished us to remain friends and stay in contact. All my concerns melted away, and I felt completely at peace. I could not have asked for more nor dreamed a more beautiful dream. I was in Heaven. My faith was rock solid, and I believed with all my heart in the beauty of this magical world.

After changing my money at the bank, I returned my rental car with 366.39 miles of Vancouver touring to show for my experience. At 1:59 pm, I boarded Continental Flight 1760, a DC-9 headed for Spokane, Washington, and we took to the air at 2:25 pm. I bid a fond farewell to Vancouver, as it slipped away beneath me. After several transfers, I finally made it home at 11:14 pm that night and officially closed out my trip log. What an adventure! This Moose Hunting excursion was truly a miraculous and blessed journey. It had surpassed all expectations and can only be explained with references to divine intervention. There could be absolutely no doubt that God had a hand in making this dream come true. I am forever grateful!

Chapter Twelve

WAR AND LOVE

R eturning to Kansas, my mind was racing about, constantly replaying moments from Vancouver and memories from Spain and eight years of questing. It was not long after my return that I was sitting back on SAC Alert and busy at work. I really just wanted a few weeks of quiet reflection, but the opportunity was not there. I had taken my ten days of leave, and it was time to get back into action. My mind dreamed on, while the passing of time brought me closer to my October 9th deployment departure date to the Pacific. I worked very hard to perfect my navigation skills, as I knew I would need them to traverse the vast expanses of the Pacific and for what I presumed was a lead-in to the inevitable combat operations in the Middle East.

Our Pacific Tanker Task Force deployment, much to my surprise, executed as scheduled. The trip encompassed some of the most challenging flying I had ever done since it was all over-water navigation, and the normal mathematical formulas changed in Southern latitudes and Eastern longitudes. Additionally, the flying weather was horrific. We flew multiple ten-plus hour flights, back and forth between Guam and Diego Garcia. These missions were spent continually dodging major thunderstorms while Saint Elmo's fire danced across the windscreen. As the navigator, I was primarily responsible for weather avoidance. I kept very busy. In the near-continuous light-to-moderate turbulence, I clung to the hand-grips, balancing myself on the sextant stool, as I tried to take celestial sightings from the aircraft sextant. I was always hoping for breaks in the clouds that might allow me to view a star or planet. These flights were completely exhausting. It seemed we were barely rested from one sortie before we were headed back through the same awful weather we had dodged on the previous leg. Back and forth we went. While deployed, we also received another briefing from the SAC Intelligence Briefing Team. The brief highlighted a very frightening assessment statistic—the estimated twenty to thirty percent losses in the tanker force during the first two nights of a war with Iraq. During the briefing, many of us looked to our left and to our right as we considered the numbers. The unspoken message: "one of us isn't coming home."

We were truly expecting to stay on at Diego Garcia for a full 180 days. So, my crew and I were very surprised when, at the end of our forty-five days, we were redeployed as originally scheduled. By mid-November, we were back in Wichita, Kansas. Upon our return, we were immediately placed back on SAC Alert.

Although I was not expecting to have an opportunity to take leave anytime soon, when I discovered I would be off Alert for Thanksgiving, I decided to seize an opportunity to head home to New York. I was not sure when, or if, the opportunity would present itself again.

The day after Thanksgiving was spent Moose Hunting in Manhattan with my brother, John. Besides seeing some traditional holiday sights (Macy's and Rockefeller Center), we visited the Dorothy Hamill poster outside Madison Square Garden and retraced our steps at the New York City Public Library, recreating our glorious adventure to look through British Columbia phone books back in 1982. It was an emotion-filled visit. We also stopped at Grand Central Terminal and visited the spot where my great adventure to Riverside, Connecticut began. While on this journey into Manhattan, I visited a book store and managed to finally find a copy of *Le Morte d'Arthur* by Thomas Mallory. The book would later accompany me to war.

Beyond the wonderful day in the City with my brother, I also took time out during my brief vacation to enjoy autumn in my hometown. My long walks took me to many special places, and I relived many special memories.

While home, I was able to help Mom celebrate her birthday. After this, it was back to Kansas and an unknown future. At work, we were all advised that war was imminent and that we all needed to be prepared to deploy on short notice. In short, "keep your bags packed and be ready."

Much to my surprise, after a month of what seemed like non-stop SAC Alert, my crew was able to take its scheduled ten days of leave. So, I headed back to New York again. The trip was very inspirational, and I spent great amounts of time wandering about in the cold and Moose Hunting. Also, I finally recovered my green rubber ball from my brother. He had been using this relic as an exercise squeeze ball, much to my horror. With the ball back in my possession, I made sure it would never again be disrespected. It may seem like a silly thing, but the image of bouncing that ball on the ferry deck during our return trip to Spain, in 1982, was a powerful memory. The ball needed to be preserved and afforded proper honors.

The famous green rubber ball

After my leave, I returned to Kansas. The next time I left, it would be the real thing. I had made it very clear that I wanted to get into the action. In fact, I still remember an Alert tour where I was sitting in the hallway with my crew prior to the morning briefing. I saw my Operations Officer walking towards us, and I jumped up and told him that I wanted to deploy. The rest of my crew made it very clear that "it's our navigator who wants to deploy, not the crew."

On January 16, 1991, my diary entry opened dramatically:

Throw all plans out the window—I'm now in crew rest for a surprise late-night mission and I don't know where to but all indications are Saudi Arabia. Won't know for sure though until I report in at 10pm tonight.

Later in the evening, I received a phone call from my co-pilot as I was lying in bed resting—he told me to turn on the television—we were at war! I ran out to my living room and was amazed at the spectacle playing out before my eyes. We were, in fact, launching an impressive array of airstrikes against Iraq. I grew even more excited about the evening mission. As it turns out, my excitement was only partially founded. We did not deploy to the combat zone that night. We did, however, have a very exciting covert mission to refuel a group of F-117 Stealth Fighters heading out to the war zone. When we arrived, we were briefed into the program and told we could not speak about, or otherwise describe, anything we were about to see that night. The mission turned out to be rather exciting, as we had an emergency shortly after takeoff—we could not raise the landing gear. We knew we couldn't continue the mission in this configuration so we declared the emergency, dumped fuel, and returned to base. When we landed, the spare jet was already waiting, ready for us. In one of the quickest "bag drags" of my career, we scrambled to the new jet, quickly ran the remaining checklists items, and were off upon our classified mission. It was very exciting! The stealthy F-117 Nighthawks did not disappoint. They were amazing! Our mission finally recovered back to McConnell AFB after 11:00 am the next morning. After landing, we found out the pilots had a check-ride the next day, so we had to mission plan for that flight. It all worked out well in the end, but I was still in Kansas—not where I wanted to be. I continued on SAC Alert and resumed reading my various knight books. My trip to Vancouver had completely cleansed my soul, and I was ready for whatever fate might have in store. My continued reading of the literature of knighthood helped to cement the powerful feelings in my heart.

I could not help but wonder if my time upon this earth was nearing an end. After all, I had completed my great quest; and there seemed little else to do besides go to war to end the injustices of an evil dictator. Feeling somewhat fatalistic, I put down a lot of money on a brand new stereo system—actually, the first stereo I had ever owned. If I was going to get blown up, I might as well enjoy a week or two of good music. I bought the system on January 23rd. A couple of days later, on January 25th, I received the notification I had desperately been waiting for. My time had come to go to war.

I was notified by my operations officer that I would be part of an all-volunteer crew heading out to the Middle East and into combat. A volunteer co-pilot from another crew and I got teamed up with a Standardization/Evaluation Pilot and Boom Operator to form the new crew. The navigator and co-pilot from the Standardization/Evaluation crew did not want to deploy and thus the two vacancies were created for me and my USAFA classmate, Ken Tucker. I was psyched! I also got very busy. There was much to do. I notified my family back in New York, and they were not at all pleased. They were also upset that I had volunteered for the deployment. That was not to be helped. I had to follow my own path. Besides, I was not deploying with the intent to die. I was cognizant of the possibility that I might not return; but I owed it to my crew, and the mission, to do everything within my power to bring my brothers in arms and our jet home safely.

January 26, 1991:

My life has been a good one and I have few regrets—to go now would not be any great tragedy though by no means do I go into battle with the intention not to return. I just realize it is a possibility and I would hope my death would not be defamed by worthless chatter of being "cut off in my prime." Bullshit! I have had a good, a pure, and a fulfilling life. There aren't a lot of things I had listed yet to do and I have done much. Yet—there are always targets of opportunity—and I am not sure my job in this world is yet done—"I know I've got one thing I've got to do—Ramble On." There are people who need help and if I may help them (if I can?) then perhaps my time on this earth is to be longer. I'll not question destiny—I shall accept it—but, by God, I am a fighting man and I'll not surrender.

On January 27th, the New York Giants won the Super Bowl in an incredible game, and I couldn't help but feel like all loose ends were getting neatly tied together.

Our adventure truly began on February 4th, the first leg of our deployment. The mission was a short hop up to Grand Forks AFB, North Dakota, to pick-up some deploying personnel. The send-off from McConnell Air Force Base was less than glamorous. Even though other bases were giving their members elaborate send-off celebrations, ours somehow felt the need to keep things very much under wraps. We were visited by the wing commander at the jet. I was having a problem with the aircraft sextant, and the wing commander seemed irritated that our departure was delayed. He wanted us to fix our problem at Grand Forks. That seemed unfathomable. As it turns out, it's fortunate we didn't take that advice. The maintenance team discovered that the entire sextant mount had been misaligned by about ten degrees while the jet was in depot. That would have impacted every heading shot I tried to take during the upcoming flights. I'm glad I discovered this during the pre-flight and that we had it repaired. The wing commander didn't wait around to see us off. It was irrelevant. Our send-off from Grand Forks, the next day, was a much nicer one. I remember it like it was yesterday. As we were taxiing out to the runway, I saw a line of snowplows driving by our jet—all the snowplows assigned to the base. They then each rolled out so that they formed a line of parallel parked vehicles along the side of the taxiway. As we rolled by, they simultaneously all raised their shovels to salute us. It was very cool. As we took off, voices came over the tower radio frequency wishing us good luck and Godspeed upon our journey. Now that's a sendoff!

The next leg of our deployment trip took us to Moron Air Base, Spain for some radio modifications to the aircraft. After this, we pushed on to RAF Mildenhall, in England. The following day, we departed from damp and chilly England; and I was thanking my lucky stars, literally, that I had the sextant fixed back in Kansas. Shortly after takeoff, I lost my Inertial Navigation System computer. Very soon afterward, the radar failed; and our Doppler Navigation System position was quickly drifting off into the weeds. I had to work my tail off to get us down to our final destination, Masirah Air Base, Oman. I relied heavily upon celestial navigation and dead reckoning to get us there. The flight over Egypt was memorable. We got to fly along the Nile River Valley and see the pyramids. Finally, on February 6th, we arrived at Masirah Air Base, Oman, which the crews affectionately called Moon Island since its barren surface reminded us all of the lunar landscape. Several days later, I was flying my first combat mission. I was at war, and yet I was at peace.

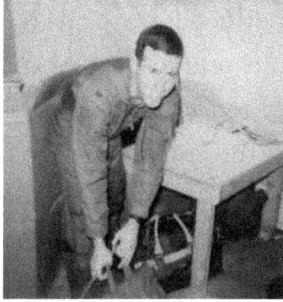

Initial arrival in "Tent City," Masirah, Oman, Operation Desert Storm

My Desert Storm flight crew

I could recount the many missions. I could tell stories of flames, fireballs and explosions, of danger and life-threatening "near misses." I could tell of teamwork and of camaraderie. I could talk about exhaustion, lousy food, months spent sleeping on a cot in a tent, hideous camel spiders stalking about, and a thousand other things. But all of this would take me off-topic. Instead, I'll mention hours spent reading, and eventually finishing, *Le Morte d'Arthur*, under the dim, flickering, light of an incandescent bulb in our tent. Then there were walks about a purposefully darkened tent city at night where the desert winds whipped the canvas tent fabric about in a scene reminiscent of an age long ago where warring armies pitched tents out in the desert. Also, the flapping tent canvas, along with the creaking tent poles and ropes, created an auditory sensation not so different from being upon an old sailing ship. So many thoughts raced through my mind. But, through it all, I stayed focused on the mission and focused upon my calling. I felt like a knight.

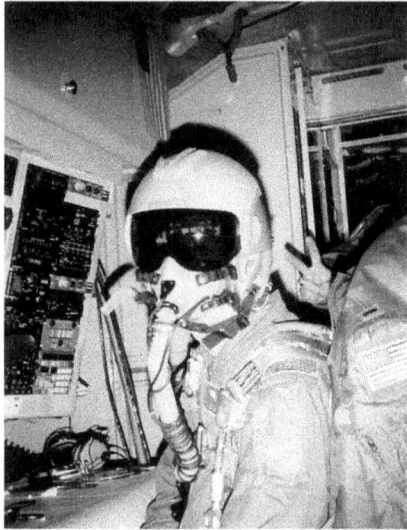

Wearing my helmet and parachute prior to "heading north" Into Iraq, Operation Desert Storm

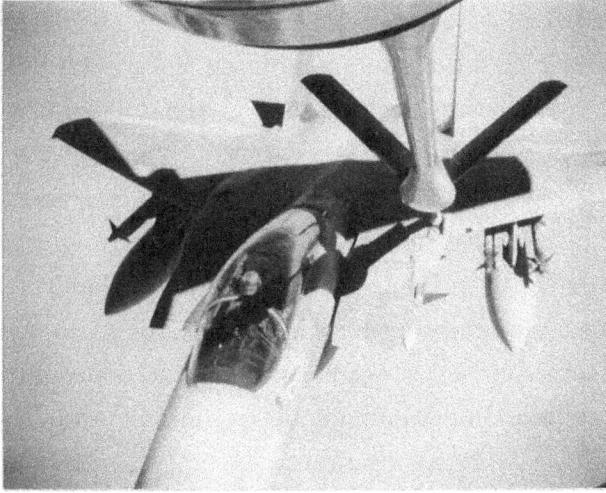

Refueling an F-15 Eagle during Operation Desert Storm

F-16 Fighting Falcon hanging off our right wing, Operation Desert Storm

A ceasefire brought an end to hostilities on February 28, 1991— the war was over. A few days later, my crew stretched the rules, just a little bit, to do a victory fly-by over our tent city. The Brits had been buzzing our tents for weeks with their Jaguars, and it was time for a little U.S. morale building. We got mildly chastised by the squadron commander after we landed our jet, but it was well worth it. We received a hero's welcome upon returning to Tent City, and I believe our little escapade helped to further enhance the morale of all Americans living there at Masirah.

Eventually, all the C-130 crews departed the island, and just the tankers and support troops remained. Missions continued but at a much lesser frequency. When all was said and done, our unit won an Outstanding Unit Award for being the only refueling unit in theater with a 100% on-time mission complete record. We were very proud of that fact. I had to note in my diary that, on March 30th, my sister got to see Dorothy Hamill skate at the University of Michigan. On that night, by coincidence, we got assigned to fly on one of the two Loring AFB jets on station. It was our first time flying a Loring jet. The tail flash was a moose. How appropriate.

It's funny now as I read through my old diary volumes. Life-threatening events were casually mentioned and have since been totally forgotten. On April 4th, I wrote about an emergency abort during takeoff, as a large flock of gulls flew over the runway. We had to pull back the throttles, get on the brakes, and then taxi back to see if we took any significant bird strikes. Had we been going a little faster, we could have very well taken birds in the engines. The resulting catastrophic engine failures, especially at our fuel-laden heavy gross weight, might very well have resulted in the loss of our aircraft and all souls onboard. I casually mention the event and then move on. Such was the life of a young aviator. Likewise, a near mid-air collision with an A-10 fighter that blasted through our altitude directly ahead of us one night, completely filling our windscreen, barely merited mention—a second of time was literally all that stood between us and a fiery death. I can still see the top of that pilot's helmet, and I will never forget the stunned silence in our cockpit as we processed just how close we all came to dying.

April 6, 1991. Our tent mates, Crew R-109, returned from a mission to Spain. While there, they had an opportunity to do some shopping. I had asked my friend to pick up several items to include cough syrup to help combat the worsening cough I had been plagued with for weeks. He fell through with most of my requests but did purchase, for himself, a small statuette that he described to me as a conquistador. That was no conquistador. I instantly recognized the Golden Helmet of Mambrino and knew that he had actually acquired a little Don Quixote statuette. I thought that was very cool. Since the crew had gone to Sevilla, a very special city in my heart, I asked about his visit to the town (where I had first fallen in love with Valerie) and inquired if, by chance, he had picked up any coins in Sevilla that he would be willing to part with. He did, and the coin he first handed me was none other than a coin dated 1982! Even in the deserts of Oman, miracles can reach the faithful. I was inspired, to put it mildly.

Relaxing between missions, Operation Desert Storm

On Masirah, missions continued with no sign of a redeployment on the horizon, even though rumors continually spread throughout the force. With the hostilities over, we flew to keep the peace; and we took cameras and binoculars to survey the lingering remnants of the destructive war we had just waged upon Iraq.

On April 15th, my diary recounts one tale of viewing the destruction:

Cool day. Got up to fly at a reasonable time—0650 show. Great flight. Up to Iraq again but the real cool part came during the return. We decided—hey, let's go down and fly over Kuwait City at 15,000. Well, we got down then we heard another aircraft request to do it at 10,000 ft. So, we figured, why not ask for 11,000—we did. Then Glen (our aircraft commander) thought—why not just go down to 5,000 ft for some super photos. So, we requested it and got that approved. Glen went into the boom pod in the back to get some photos leaving me and Ken alone in the cockpit. Well, the radar controller (Approach) got to talking with us saying how today wasn't the best day for sight-seeing as it was really smoky. Then, much to our amusement, he offered to set us up for a PAR approach to Kuwait International Airport—to go all the way down to 1,000 ft! We tried to get Glen in back but he and the Boom were off headset—so, us two 1st Lts consulted each other and made a command decision to go for it! We started down. I figured I had better alert Glen of what we were doing. [After I checked off headset to go in back and tell him], Glen rocketed up to the front of the aircraft but when he found out the controller had suggested it (possibly to check his equipment), Glen was as psyched as we were. Thus, were we vectored about—the destruction and fireballs/fire spouts larger than life from only 1000 ft. And, finally, we got vectored right over the runway. You can simply not ask for better—amazing!!! I took several photos with my cheapo camera which ought to turn out pretty good— I hope. What a flight!"

I still remember this as the most spectacular flight of my life. It felt like flying through Hell as we slowly maneuvered around the towering pillars of flame while oil went streaming across our aircraft's windscreen. Things seemed to move in slow motion. It was truly incredible!

Flying towards the oil field fires in Kuwait, Operation
Desert Storm

On April 24th, I finally completed reading all of Malory's *Le Morte d'Arthur*. Now, I was ready for home. On the flight that day, my Aircraft Commander permitted me to fly the entire approach from 27,000 ft. down to and including landing the jet on the airstrip at Masirah! I was thrilled to be at the controls again! A few days later, we received reports of a massive tornado that had struck our home base, McConnell AFB. Reports continued to come in throughout the day, and the devastation was clearly immense. Many of us wondered what things were going to look like when we finally did get to return. I was also concerned about my truck, which I had left parked at the squadron. Amidst all of the commotion, we at Masirah remained the forgotten ones. It turns out we were the only aircrew members still living in tents in the theater. They even stopped our mail—someone simply thought that our base had closed. There was a little excitement towards the end as they discovered an active Surface to Air Missile site right beneath the track where we had been orbiting on nearly a daily basis. That little fact quickly got our attention. Iraq was still a dangerous place.

Gradually, our desert home was dismantled. The eventual departure was far less glorious than one might have hoped for. The chow hall closed so we ate Meals Ready to Eat (MREs). The sleeping bags were packed away, so we slept on empty army cots. The lull in activity as we waited for the fabled L-1011 charter flight to take us away allowed me the opportunity to reflect on the experience in my diary and calculate a few final statistics of my crew's performance during the war. I determined that, during the war, my crew offloaded a total of 3,298,900 lbs. of fuel (approximately 492,373 gallons). We were all pretty proud of the missions we flew and the contributions to the war and liberation of Kuwait.

Our tent on "Moon Island," Operation Desert Storm

Despite early feelings of betrayal, being directed to fly a chartered commercial aircraft back home rather than gloriously returning in our own jet, the return flight turned out to be something very special. On May 9th, we woke up at 0330 and did our final packing and tent cleaning. We all made our way down to the Maintenance Hangar at 0430, anticipating a rather long wait before our departure. The timing worked out better than expected. At 0541, our L-1011 lifted off and wild cheers reverberated throughout the aircraft—it was very reminiscent of videos I had once seen of Vietnam War POWs on their way home following repatriation. The diarrhea that plagued me that morning could not dampen my spirits. Our return trip took us through Cairo, Egypt; Shannon, Ireland; Bangor, Maine; Charleston, South Carolina; and, finally, to Malmstrom Air Force Base in Montana. We watched patriotic videos, saw numerous movies, and had some pretty good meals served up. Ireland was great! After over three months of seeing nothing but sand brown, the brilliant green of an Irish spring was nothing short of miraculous. My crew treated me to an Irish Coffee at the Shannon Airport. It was the last alcoholic drink I've consumed. The coffee was terrific. I joke around in my diary about not having enough time to find a wife...but you know I had my eyes open. There was no way to know that our next stop would out-shine even our fun-filled refueling break in Ireland. Bangor would surpass Shannon in a very significant and meaningful way.

Crossing over so many time zones on our global excursion, I really had no idea what time of day it was. It was suggested that we might want to shave prior to landing in Bangor, if we had a razor available. Since I had my electric shaving razor with me, I went into the airplane's lavatory and cleaned up a bit.

When the airplane door opened at the gate in Bangor, I could hardly believe my ears. I could have sworn I heard band music playing. I was not mistaken. I didn't know it at the time, but the good people of Bangor had dedicated themselves to greeting every arriving jet carrying troops returning from the war. The welcome was nothing short of eye-watering. We came off the jet and were ushered between two endless lines of well-wishers, all wanting to shake our hands, hug us, and welcome us home. Little flags and gifts were provided by some. It seemed like the entire town was there at the airport. From my diary:

> It was an eye-watering experience when we got off that jet—it looked like nearly the whole town showed up to greet us—patriotic music played and people cheered—it was packed. A huge receiving line stretched through the airport—I must have shaken several hundred hands and got several hugs from young and old and many veterans. We were asked by many to sign books and T-Shirts and they gave us flags, teddy bears, yellow ribbons, cookies and lots of other nice welcoming presents. It was wonderful and made everything worthwhile—made me glad we got stuck on that L-1011. A marine contingent arrived just after us. Then, we all celebrated. Man—what a fantastic hero's welcome! It was truly a heartwarming and joyous occasion—thank you Bangor!

Perhaps the most beautiful part of the Bangor welcome came towards the end. A group of veterans stood up on a stage and asked if anyone from our group was also a veteran of the Vietnam War. Only one person was, the Colonel who had been our commanding officer on Masirah. The vets asked him to come forward. They gave him a hug and said that they wanted to give him a special welcome to make up for the welcome he never received when returning from Vietnam. The Colonel broke out in tears...and most of us did, too. Yes! I will never forget the good people of Bangor, Maine, and how they made us feel upon our return from Desert Storm...and Vietnam.

We eventually made our way back onto the aircraft for the leg down to Charleston, South Carolina, where we offloaded the majority of our passengers. After a brief delay, we continued on to our final destination for this flight—Malmstrom AFB, Montana. We landed there at 11:53 pm (local time). We finally reached our hotel, The Ponderosa Hotel, at 1:55 am. We were tired. Very tired. What do I remember about that experience? I remember the second-best shower of my life. The first being that shower after returning from the woods in Survival Training. It felt so nice to take a long, warm, shower in a real bathroom rather than in the drippy, sand-covered, open bay showers of Masirah.

The next morning after breakfast, a McConnell AFB jet arrived to pick us up and take us all home. We landed at McConnell at 2:33 pm on May 10th, concluding our ninety-six day Desert Storm deployment. They did have a little welcome for us at McConnell, but it was very anticlimactic after the incredible welcome at Bangor. My co-pilot and I toured around the base looking at all the destruction wreaked by the tornado—it still looked like a complete disaster zone. Unfortunately, Ken's sailboat, which had been parked in the RV lot, had taken a lot of damage. Over a hundred houses in base housing had been destroyed or severely damaged. The one saving grace is that no one was killed on McConnell. Tragically, the good folks of Andover, Kansas, the twister's next touchpoint, were not so lucky. It was an incredibly powerful and devastating tornado.

I eventually returned to my apartment. It was quiet. The war was over. I reflected upon those initial intelligence reports of massive losses to our tanker force. I reflected upon my visit to Vancouver and reunion with Valerie. All the pieces seemed to be laid out for a noble demise in a just war. To me, it seemed like the packaging was complete. But God kept me around. It was not my time. I was prepared to die. I felt at peace with myself and my life. I was ready. But, God was not ready to have me leave this world yet. I had to wonder why. I knew better than to ever question God's judgment. I knew I had to make good on my new lease on life. I had no idea what to expect or even what to hope for, as I began this next chapter in my life.

Chapter Thirteen

THE NEXT FIFTEEN

September 10, 1990, was the last time I ever spoke with Valerie. Nothing can change that fact. But the following years were not without inspiration and magic and stories that very much relate to my Lady Valerie.

In August of 1991, my crew was selected to participate in an airshow at McChord Air Force Base, Washington. While there, on our day off, I was able to rent a car and return for a brief visit to Vancouver. My time was very limited; and while I thought long and hard about trying to make contact with Valerie, it just seemed like things would be too rushed. I wasn't sure if she would still be there, since she had previously explained how she moved around a lot. Also, I knew that any meeting would necessarily be rushed and Valerie deserved much better—she deserved all of my time, should she desire it. Finally, there was a part of me that didn't want to risk messing up the ending to what seemed like a very lovely story. I did drive by many of the special places that had great meaning for me, to include the spot outside Shenanigan's where I last gazed upon my lady. It was a beautiful Moose Hunting adventure. It was also the last time I would travel to Vancouver as a single man.

Over the coming years, I would get married, move to numerous bases, and change my Air Force job title countless times. Through it all, a constant thread remained—Valerie and my faith. The two bound the days, weeks, months, and years together in one magical continuum. If you'll forgive me for jumping around through time, I'd like to share a few special stories from the fifteen years following my return from the war.

December 14, 1992. While on Temporary Duty (TDY) in South Dakota, attending the Joint Employment Tactics School, I was having a difficult and somewhat lonely trip. At 4:40 am, I was awakened by what I thought was an alarm—but it wasn't mine. It may well be that I was dreaming, but it all seemed quite real. I heard a voice in the darkness asking me if I still believed. I said, "Yes...thank you." The voice returned and said, "You're welcome." I felt very inspired. This all seemed quite amazing. Eventually, I drifted back to sleep and awoke at 6:30 am. I may never know for sure whether or not I was dreaming; but regardless, the inspiration in my heart now was very real.

On January 7, 1993, I worked up the courage to ask my future wife out for a date. To my surprise, she said yes. I was ecstatic, but there was still a part of me that wondered if I was not diverging off the path that was set before me. At the time, I was just happy to find a woman who was interested in spending some time with me. I was fairly used to being invisible and had grown accustomed to it. It was nice to be noticed. I was happy. Lisa and I had three quick dates before the time came for me to deploy to Moron Air Base, Spain, to support operation Restore Hope—the famine relief effort in Somalia.

While in Spain, I had a wonderful opportunity to spend a day off in Sevilla. I hung out with my crew for a while and finally broke away for some Moose Hunting. It was the first time I had been back since Valerie and I had been there together in 1982. The memories and the feelings came flooding back.

I eventually returned from that trip and picked up where I left off with Lisa. It seemed our entire relationship was filled with a never-ending stream of deployments and TDYs. In April, only four months after having met Lisa, I decided to ask her to marry me; and in August of 1993, we tied the knot. Even with this happiness, there remained part of me that did not want to let go. As I donned my mess dress and prepared to leave my apartment for the Wichita Botanical Gardens where we were to be married, I felt a need to play "Ramble On" one last time—a sort of final act of defiance. I cranked up my stereo all the way; and the walls trembled as the music played, and I sang along as loudly as I could. The preceding eleven years were a very special part of my life, and I wasn't quite ready yet to box it all up and store these cherished memories in the dark corner of an attic. However, I also felt that Lisa deserved my undivided attention and loyalty—wasn't that part of being a good husband? Wasn't that my new duty? I was confused...but I was also minutes away from taking wedding vows. We did get married, by Judge Corrigan, on that 18th day of August, 1993. Our honeymoon was a beautiful Alaskan Inside Passage Cruise. It was not lost on me that the starting point for this cruise was Vancouver, Canada. As our cab drove through the streets of the city, familiar street names and places still struck a chord with me.

In the summer of 1994, we moved down to Altus, Oklahoma, where I was newly assigned as a Combat Crew Training School instructor navigator. While I was not overly fond of Altus, the job of training students how to fly tankers was a terrifically rewarding experience which I greatly enjoyed. In 1996, after several years of trying, we were finally blessed with our first child, Thomas Arthur

Lange. I chose the first name from the character of the young boy at the end of the play *Camelot*. As King Arthur's dream falls to ruin, he shares his story with this young boy, knights him, and bids him to flee to safety behind the lines and tell the tale of the beauty that once was his noble kingdom. Tommy's middle name was, of course, in honor of the great king of legend, King Arthur.

My days were not without stress, and I found myself slowly drifting away from the beliefs that had been so foundational for me. But, just as in times of old, God and the angels came to my rescue with a brilliant sign—a miracle. Allow me to relay the story of April 25, 1997, just as I wrote it in my diary that day:

> Mark this day! I have news to pass of another one of those small miracles that occurred just moments ago. As you know, my "energy" or passion for the Great Cause has not been very high lately but just now something amazing happened—a sign!
>
> I had just taken my shower and was debating whether or not to draw the sword this morning. After moments of reflection, I elected not to—after all, what was the point? This was a sad state of affairs. But, just as I had turned from my sword, I heard a loud crashing sound—it came from the dark corner of my bedroom, by the bookshelf. I couldn't see what had happened but I guessed something must have fallen off of the bookcase. The sound had occurred just as I had turned from my sword, deciding not to draw it today. I got my flashlight and shone it at the bookcase and then at the floor nearby. It was my mini-sword rack that I had gotten back in Spain in 1982! I believe the 8 little metal swords were probably designed for hors d'oeuvres but that, obviously, is not why I got it. It stands about 3 to 4 inches tall. Something had caused it to come flying off the bookcase just as I had made my inappropriate decision. The swords did not stay with the stand but were, amazingly, scattered all over the floor for several feet in all directions. The only thing I can figure is one book must have "slipped"

out of place to knock it off but I have no doubt it was a sign from my guardian angels for so clear was its meaning and symbolism. My heart and soul filled just as wind fills the sails of a doldrums-plagued ship to bring new life. I immediately turned to my sword and drew it with a full heart. I had so needed a sign and on this misty, rainy, mystical day it came to me in an indisputable fashion. Perhaps 'twas a book that pushed the swords but 'twas then no mortal force that pushed the book which had, for months, remained rock-steady in that place. I believe! Thank you!"

In the coming days, I reviewed the forensics of the scene. There was no sign of a book strike and there was no way a sliding book could have propelled the sword rack in such a way as to spread them halfway across the room and in so many directions. I needed no more proof that God was continuing to look out for this poor knight. It wasn't very long after that I committed myself to a new battle to reaffirm my faith and strengthen my dedication to God and the Cause. In fact, the very next morning, I laid upon my dresser the eight swords which had fallen from my sword rack and drew the first, beginning what would be an eight-week battle, appropriately called "The Great Battle of the Eight Sword Miracle!"

Mini-sword display rack on my bookshelf

In August of 1997, we were off on our next assignment—to Royal Air Force Base Mildenhall, in England. I was very excited to be moving overseas, especially to England. The move was certainly filled with logistical challenges, all of which we success-fully overcame. We lived off base for our first year and a half before finally getting an on-base residence, on RAF Lakenheath (a quick drive from my workplace at RAF Mildenhall). This move occurred shortly after the birth of our daughter, Rebecca. Rebecca was born in January of 1999. She was named after Rebecca from *Ivanhoe* and her middle name, Lynn, was a shortened form of

Lynette, inspired by the character from "Sir Gawain and the Green Knight."

Taking a celestial shot using the aircraft's periscopic sextant

While in England, I was blessed with another chance to visit Spain again—this time as part of a Presidential Support Mission. On this trip, besides visiting Sevilla, I also got to do some extended Moose Hunting. Having a few days off, I managed to talk several friends into joining me on excursions to Torremolinos (March 26, 1998) and Granada and the Alhambra (March 27th). Both locations carried very special meaning for me. While touring about, I ensured we visited several of the special places that had strong associations with Valerie.

In Torremolinos, we walked the same pedestrian shopping street where I had seen Valerie and where I had purchased my knight statue. More significantly, we made a detour to the Hotel Cervantes. My friends were, doubtless, wondering why we were stopping there. I didn't bother trying to explain. Inside the hotel, I stood silently in the lobby. Over there! It was over there where I sat for hours, awaiting the arrival of my Lady Valerie. I didn't see her that afternoon; but oh, the daydreams I had! My crew had already seen all they needed to of the hotel lobby and were heading out as I snapped a photo or two. When I exited, one of my very good friends and fellow navigator asked if he could take my picture in front of the hotel. He said he didn't know why, but he could tell the hotel was a very special place for me. Although still quite camera shy in those days, I agreed to the photo. That photograph is, to this day, one of my very favorites. It captured me "armored up" and in the euphoric state that only a magical Moose Hunting adventure can produce. More than any other photo I have—that picture truly captures who I am.

Standing in front of the Hotel Cervantes, Torremolinos,
Spain (March 26, 1998)

Although we were too late to get into the gardens, our visit to the Alhambra and Granada was also very inspirational. Together, these Spanish excursions were a remarkably beautiful experience. I returned to England with added inspiration in my heart.

By all accounts, my tour in England was an enjoyable and successful one. I was selected to represent our wing at the 1998 Airlift Rodeo flying competition, and I was also awarded the Institute of Navigation Superior Achievement Award for 1998 which was an incredible honor. I traveled with my family to Massachusetts to receive the award.

In the spring of 1999, I got to see combat again in Operation Allied Force (March 24, 1999–June 10, 1999). It had been several years since I had flown wartime missions; but in our unit, I was one of the few fliers who had actual combat experience.

Navigating the KC-135R on an "Airlift Rodeo" flying competition sortie

Receiving the 1998 Institute of Navigation Superior Achievement Award From the Institute of Navigation president

I helped plan missions and briefed crews; when possible, I also signed up to fly combat sorties. It was an exciting time. In fact, one of the most memorable moments of my Air Force career happened during this conflict. I was up flying one night when, over our secure radio, I heard that an American F-117 Stealth Fighter had been shot down. The pilot had ejected and was on the ground, desperately trying to evade capture by the enemy. We were already at our "BINGO" fuel. That means it's time to go back home before your gas gauge is sitting on "E." Okay, we don't really have an "E" on our fuel gauges, but the concept is the same. I was the navigator on the number two tanker of our two-ship formation. Lead had several thousand pounds of fuel more than us in his tanks and was starting to work our clearance out of the area and back to England. I knew we had to stay. We were equipped with a drogue that night (capable of refueling U.S. Navy and NATO receivers), and I knew many of the tankers currently in the air were only boom refueling capable (primarily U.S. fighters and bombers). I began working math like a madman and was crunching numbers as quickly as I could. Before the mission began, I had printed off all the wind charts over Europe for multiple altitudes, and I noticed an anomaly at the higher altitudes on this particular night that would help us on our journey back. I quickly told the aircraft commander that I was highly confident that we could stay on station for at least one more hour. Trust is essential in our business, and I was very glad that the crew trusted me. It didn't hurt that I was a seasoned instructor navigator and had previously been an instructor and evaluator at the tanker Combat Crew Training School. We radioed up to lead and told him that we were staying. Since we had less fuel than the lead tanker, we basically shamed him into canceling his departure clearance, as well. We both stayed; shortly after, two Navy EA-6B electronic jamming aircraft were vectored to us for gas. These aircraft would play a critical role in opening up the corridor for the recovery package to fight their way in towards our downed pilot. The story goes on from there, but the best part is at the end —as we were making our way back towards our recovery base, we heard the call we had all been praying for—the F-117 pilot was safely recovered by the Combat Search and Rescue team. That was a great Air Force day! The conflict ended on June 10, 1999, and peace was restored in Europe.

While stationed in England, I was promoted to the rank of major and finished out my assignment as a flight commander— the Chief of Plans and Tactics. It seemed our time in England went by so quickly. Before we knew it, it was time to move again. Knowing that the days of the navigator were growing numbered in the KC-135, thanks to the PACER CRAG avionics "upgrade," I decided to try my luck and put in an application package for a Special Duty Assignment. Much to my joy, I was selected to join the elite team flying the E-4B National Airborne Operations Center (NAOC). I was thrilled! This also meant we'd be assigned to a base just four hours away from my wife's hometown. Lisa was happy about this assignment, too.

I reported in with the 1st Airborne Command and Control Squadron at Offutt Air Force Base, Nebraska in the summer of 2000 and quickly got checked out as a navigator in the E-4B. Not many months later, my second daughter, Kathleen, was born on a very special Halloween night.

August 25, 2001. In the mail, I received a birthday gift from my sister—a small skating moose statuette wearing a Canadian sweat-shirt. The gift seemed very appropriate.

Boeing E-4B in flight

Sitting at my navigator station on the E-4B

More amazingly, that night, on a lark, I decided one more time to do an online search for the name Valerie Dudoward. Much to my amazement, a website came up with a yearly review for native counselors in British Columbia. And on that website, I saw a current picture of Valerie. I was thrilled. What a wonderful birthday gift. What perfect timing!

In 2002, I was selected to attend Air Command and Staff College at Maxwell Air Force Base, Alabama. Sadly, I had to leave a job I loved, flying the E-4B. However, I knew that going to school was the right thing to do. We spent a year at Maxwell AFB, in Montgomery, Alabama, before eventually returning to Offutt AFB, Nebraska, and a new job working in the Headquarters for United States Strategic Command. On September 5, 2003, our final child, Henry Lange, was born. I cannot imagine the family without any of the four. Our home was filled with love.

Even with four children and as a seasoned Air Force officer, I never gave up on those parts of who I was that I knew were foundational. Some might argue that I should have. Let them speculate. In the end, I shall do as I have always done and follow my heart. I held close to heart my faith and my feelings for those Friends who had inspired me to keep going when hope seemed lost. Throughout the hard times, the miracles and small "coincidences" continued to provide inspiration. These seemed to validate that my beliefs were not without merit—the magical world I believed in was something very real.

March 4, 2004. Inside, I could feel the tension between the knightly world of my dreams and my earthly world as a husband, father, and Air Force officer. This conflict was not new. I happened to stumble upon an e-mail address for Valerie (although I was fairly certain it was no longer valid). I debated whether or not to send her a note to find out how she was doing. I finally decided that I should. This decision was not reached without a certain level of soul searching. I never did receive a reply. However, my decision seems to have been validated by another small miracle that night. The event happened so late in the evening that I had to add it as a postscript to my diary entry for the day.

Many years before, as a young man, I saw an episode of the popular television western, *Bonanza*, that I fondly remembered throughout the years. This particular episode featured a Don Quixote-like character. I had only seen that episode once in my life, even though I watched numerous *Bonanza* reruns throughout the years. On the night of March 4th, as I flipped through channels before bed, I happened to stumble upon this lost *Bonanza* episode—and it was just beginning! Naturally, I watched it. And once again, an interesting and unexpected "happening" served to provide some much-needed validation for the crazy faith within my soul. My faith, in turn, sustained the best parts of who I was as a person.

As time passed, I continued to celebrate August by honoring Valerie and the Cause. Occasionally, I'd hold all-night vigils. While I loved the intense spirituality of an all-night vigil, they were physically challenging and somewhat difficult to explain to my family. My kids knew their father was going to be a little bit odd during "the Magical Month of August." They accepted that and, later, embraced it. For my part, I'd try to make August a fun time for the kids, too. I'd create elaborate interactive multi-day stories to share with my children. These stories would involve a number of characters and props and usually revolved around a make-believe good vs. evil struggle. The time we shared during these pre-bedtime escapades was very special. It was fun, but I also harbored the hope that the tales would inspire my kids to think creatively about life's challenges.

Every August I'd gather up my collected writings and memorabilia; and I'd engage anew in some Moose Hunting efforts, even if they were only local research activities.

On August 13, 2004, I received a copy of the play Valerie had written, *Teach Me the Ways of the Sacred Circle*, from an online used book store. It was written back in 1986, about four years after

Valerie's return from Spain. Without the wonders of the internet, it is unlikely I would have ever found this gem. *Teach Me...* was included in a collection with several other plays. I eagerly poured through the pages—I absolutely loved it! I could definitely feel Valerie's spirit in the words.

While a book purchase was something I could control, miracles were a wholly different matter. On September 2, 2004, I was blessed with another beautiful sign from God. Again, I will take you to the pages of my diary as I recount this beautiful experience:

> An amazing <u>miracle</u> this morning at 2:30 am—one I can find no reasonable explanation for. In the spirit of August, I have been listening to my music tapes recently—songs I taped off the radio in 1982. Well, I have no doubt I turned my tape deck off when I went to bed and I have no doubt the play button was not depressed. If it had been, the tape would have been audibly playing or have ran [sic] to a stop. At about 2:30 am, I was awakened by music. At first, I thought I was dreaming—but after several minutes, I realized I was not—my old songs were playing [songs I had taped in 1982 and that reminded me of Valerie]. I got my flashlight and walked into the office where I saw the power on and the play button depressed on my tape deck/radio. I was truly shocked. I pushed the stop button and returned to bed—but I could not sleep. Then, I can almost swear I heard the songs continuing. I was so sure, I got up again and went to my office. The power button was on on my radio, but the tape was not rolling and no sound was coming from it. I pushed the power button off and returned to bed. I did not sleep much. That tape "V" (for Valerie) should play at 2:30 am is beyond any reasonable explanation I could come up with. But, today is the anniversary of the day I finally got to speak with Valerie again—our first phone conversation on my Vancouver adventure and the first time I'd spoken with Valerie since 1982. Whatever the case—I hold this morning's events as nothing

short of a <u>miracle</u>—a reminder to me from above that there is magic in this world and I must keep faith. I must never stop believing. Thank you!

My wish tonight is that your life may be blessed by such wonders as I have seen and known.

It has been a good day.

Many of the miracles in my life were not so spectacular, but each one is special and each one is a gift. As a brief example of one (of many), I look to March 13, 2005. I was driving to the store this morning and thought to myself that I should find my Train CD when I get home and play "Calling All Angels." I felt in the mood for this song and some inspiration. Amazingly, on my return journey home from the store, which is only a five to ten-minute drive, that very song came on my car radio. This may not seem like much to the casual observer; but when added to the huge volume of such blessings I have received during my life, it becomes part of the wonderful reality that this world is, in fact, a very magical and beautiful place.

The following year, August of 2006 was something very special —it was more magical than most. In retrospect, I have to believe there was a powerful reason.

Chapter Fourteen

GOD TAKES HIS ANGEL HOME

August of 2006 began like many of the Augusts before with praise for my Lady Valerie and an anniversary battle to pay homage to my God, the Cause, and the lady who inspired me. On August 2nd, "The Great Battle of the Northern Angel" began. The title would be more appropriate than I could ever have imagined. At this time in my career, I was assigned to the United States Air Force Academy and working for the Commandant of Cadets. As it turns out, miracles and the comforting hand of God followed me up into the mountains of Colorado. On August 9, 2006, in the middle of my magical month of August, God provided me with yet another wonderful miracle to remind me.

On August 9th, I elected to grab some lunch at the Officers' Club. I rarely did this due to the expense and the added time it took to get down to the Club from the Cadet Area. When it came time to pay the cashier, I handed over my cash and received but a single coin in change. It was a nickel. However, much to my amazement, it was no ordinary nickel—the single coin resting within my palm was a Canadian nickel. I was thrilled. I held the coin tightly in my hand as I left the dining room. I considered placing the coin in my pocket, but a voice inside of me seemed to be telling me that there might be more to the story. I didn't even want to look. I was so very pleased with what had already come to pass. The urge to further investigate was irresistible. I had to answer the call. I opened my fist, gazed upon the coin safely resting in my palm, and turned it over to check out the date. I stared in disbelief. The date on the coin was 1982! My heart just soared as I exited to the parking lot. I looked up to the sky and said a very solemn "thank you." I have always believed in miracles; and on that day, I was most certainly witness to a very special and meaningful one. I have never forgotten that day nor the many times that God provided me comfort in my time of need—God and His angels.

Miraculous pocket change, August 9, 2006

Days passed and I continued my August reflection to include my traditional re-reading of the "Valerie" story I wrote upon my return from Spain. On the 15th, as I reflected upon that oh so difficult day back in 1982, I was again inspired by one of those "small coincidences" that often come my way. In the morning, as I drove to work and switched radio stations (my usual station not playing anything I was interested in), my favorite song came on the radio —"Ramble On." During the War Years, as you know, the song had been my modern-day knight-errantry anthem. It was very appropriate that it should play on the anniversary of the day I bid farewell to Valerie in Spain and also made a commitment to, one day, ramble on and "find the queen of all my dreams." The song was a special reminder.

August transitioned into September; and I continued my reflection as I mentally relived my 1990 trip to Vancouver, British Columbia. The most celebrated of my September anniversaries is, of course, September 7th. This was the day when I finally saw Valerie again, after eight years of searching, hoping, and praying. September 7, 2006, was a miraculous day in its own right. The dream I had in the early morning hours was nothing short of awe-inspiring. I now look upon this dream in a very different way—as kind of a final farewell. From my diary:

> Well, as I slept last night—actually in the early hours of this morning
> (Sept 7th), I had one of the longest and most vividly detailed dreams of
> my life—it was so very, very real. It seemed like I was spending an
> entire day up in Canada. In my dream, I visited British Columbia and
> tracked down Valerie's parents—I visited them in their very small and
> isolated cottage on what seemed to be a native aboriginal settlement. I
> met with Valerie's parents and we discussed all kinds of wonderful
> things, including Valerie. They then showed me their old photo albums
> where I searched desperately for photos of Valerie of about the age she
> was (20s) when I knew her in Spain. There were very few—most
> were of her as a child or older. It didn't seem like there were many

photos, at all. However, I finally came upon one of her from High School—close enough! She looked beautiful! I made a copy of the photo. Finally, perhaps unexpectedly, Valerie showed up and we spent many wonderful hours together talking and then walking together out in the cool, damp, British Columbia day. The scene was rather rustic —and so very peaceful. This is when I finally woke up—feeling very rested, exhilarated, and at peace. What a beautiful dream. The fact that it occurred today, on September 7th, is truly amazing and no less than miraculous! When I awoke from the dream, I immediately sat up in bed and felt this incredible rush of warmth rush through my body —just like someone had just covered me in a warm blanket. Even more amazingly, my ears both simultaneously popped when I sat up. This was a phenomenon that had never happened to me before and I could only believe that there had been some kind of spiritual presence with me there in the room. This was no normal dream—this was another miracle!

Seventeen days later, on September 24, 2006, Valerie passed away in Vancouver. The official cause of death was pneumonia. One may surmise that there was more to the equation—a broken heart, the prolonged effect of years of suffering, the neglect of an abusive relationship? Rather than question all the forensics, I can only find peace by believing that God had decided to return His angel home. Home, where she might finally find peace and dance with the rest of the angels. I did not find out about Valerie's death until November 24, 2006—on my mother's birthday. I cried for hours. My heart was devastated for weeks and months. The pain still lingers.

After I found out about Valerie's death, I left a condolence message on a web page, at the end of March, that had been created for such offerings. The message eventually made its way to Valerie's sister, Pamela, who replied back to me on March 28, 2007.

We quickly became friends as we shared memories and thoughts about Valerie. This relationship would form the centerpiece for a growing bond with the Dudoward family and a wonderful voyage of discovery where I learned about Valerie Dudoward and all the incredible accomplishments of her life—things I never knew about...things she was too modest to discuss.

Chapter Fifteen

TO HONOR A LADY

*P*am Dudoward and I continued regular e-mail contact as she informed me about upcoming plans for a dinner to honor Valerie in Prince Rupert, Canada. Prince Rupert seemed like a world away; but now, no longer a penniless teen, I had the resources to make such journeys and plans began to formulate in my head. As I intently followed the stories others told of Valerie, more connections began to materialize—more reasons to believe our relationship was more than just a chance encounter. I don't know that I needed more "aha! moments" to bolster my faith in this regard, but I'm always grateful when parts of the puzzle seem to come together. I'd like to share a story taken from my April 5, 2007, diary entry:

Pretty much since we first made contact, Pam Dudoward and I have been exchanging regular e-mails. I believe it has helped us both deal with the loss of Valerie. Last night was one of those wonderful times when I felt like there was some magic in the air. Shortly after learning of Valerie's death, I first heard the song "You're Beautiful," by James

Blunt on the radio. When I heard the song, it touched me very deeply and I actually cried as I listened. It so reminded me of Valerie and the very few moments we spent together. I've listened to that song a lot lately. I mentioned it to Pam last night and, apparently, freaked her out a little bit. She wrote me back how Valerie absolutely loved that song. She tells a story of driving her sister back from a memorial service when it came on the radio. Pam says she made a comment about getting tired of hearing it over and over on the radio and Valerie, who normally didn't raise a fuss over anything, strongly objected, reiterating that she really loved it. Pam apparently chose this song, consequently, to lead off a memorial DVD she is making to celebrate Valerie's life. For me, the notion of being so touched by a song that also struck Valerie was a very special thing. For Pam, I think she also took some special significance from this. Long ago, I stopped looking for "why" things happened—I've always just rejoiced in the fact that things were happening. My life has been blessed and I am grateful. I am so very grateful! Thank you."

A few days later, some photos of Valerie that Pam sent arrived in the mail. These were incredibly special to me. To that point, all I had was my 1982 photo with Valerie walking in the other direction, a great distance away. To see photos of Valerie from her younger years was indescribably wonderful. And then the signs started coming my way—old songs that I haven't heard in ages appearing on the radio, immediately followed by other songs that I associated with Valerie. I could feel the magic momentum building in my life. Through the lingering sadness, I felt a sense of comfort that the universe was still as I had once dreamt it to be. Order was being restored to my world.

On May 13, 2007, I departed Colorado Springs en route to Prince Rupert, Canada. It was a very long journey, and it was a costly one. None of this mattered to me—the cause was so important that I would have traveled the globe twice over, and at any cost, to be present for the tribute event honoring Valerie.

I should note that, at this time, Lisa still was unaware of the significance of this journey for me. It was a secret I never meant to keep and one I would have rapidly divulged were I ever asked. I never was.

While on my layover in Vancouver, I had the pleasure of meeting up with a few of Pam's friends, Dave and Joan Madison, who were also headed up to Prince Rupert for the occasion. They had lived there before so I enjoyed the company, a few stories about Valerie, and the primer on how to negotiate the complicated arrival process at Prince Rupert which involved collecting your bags from a drop chute, dropping your bags off on a curb to be loaded in a truck, riding a bus to catch a ferry, taking a ferry from Digby Island across the water to Prince Rupert, continuing on the bus to a hotel drop-off point, and finally retrieving your luggage off the baggage truck as it deposited the bags on the curb. Quite a process!

Air Canada flight into Prince Rupert (May 13, 2007)

The two-hour flight from Vancouver to Prince Rupert was

absolutely breathtaking. There was beautiful scenery the entire way—shoreline and snow-capped mountains. It was the most scenic flight I had ever taken.

I met back up with Dave and Joan at the airport, and we all rendezvoused with Pam Dudoward at the Highliner Hotel drop-off point. Pam drove us to our hotel, The Crest. After cleaning up a bit from our respective journeys, we all had dinner together. On this night, I also had the pleasure to meet with, albeit briefly, Valerie's mother, Ruth. I could tell right away that she was something special. Following dinner, I helped Pam set up the audiovisual equipment in the banquet room in preparation for the tribute dinner, planned for the next night.

My first visit to Prince Rupert, B.C., Canada

The following day was a pensive one. I spent a fair amount of time looking out my hotel window upon the beautiful inlet and pine-covered mountains. Snowcapped mountains towered farther in the distance. Not wishing to be confined to my room, I eventually broke away from my morning revelry and headed out to explore the town of Prince Rupert. I walked through the entire downtown area but also spent a considerable amount of time looking out on the harbor. It was so very peaceful. So beautiful. It was Valerie's town!

Prince Rupert, B.C., Canada

Prince Rupert, view along Cow Bay

I bumped into Dave and Joan during my wanderings and joined them and one of their old acquaintances at the local coffee shop, Cowpuccino's, which derived its name from the waters of Cow Bay. After this brief social time, I was off again, exploring. I eventually stopped by a sandwich shop to get a quick meal.

It wasn't until after lunch that I felt the tension starting to build within me. Weeks before, Pam had asked me if I would like to be put on the program as a speaker. I graciously thanked her but told her no. I explained that I didn't think there was any way I could stand in front of an audience of over 100 people and talk about a subject that was so incredibly emotional for me. I just knew I'd fall apart. Pam then mentioned that there would be an "open mic" throughout the night for anyone who wanted to share their stories or memories of Valerie. I didn't know if I could do this either; in my heart, I knew that half a story is no story at all. If I was going to speak at all, I would have to tell the whole story. While I did bring a few old keepsakes to potentially help get me through it, I was quite unsure, right up until the very end, whether or not I would actually have the guts to get up and say anything. I hadn't slept much the night before; my mind was dwelling heavily upon the upcoming event.

So there I was. Speakers were coming to the microphone and telling their short stories and sharing memories. I sat, stomach churning, in my seat, with a bag of keepsakes hidden out of sight beneath the table. The speakers, planned and impromptu, were all wonderful. At my table sat a young lady who was Valerie's great-niece, Ravan. Ravan was to have a speaking part later in the program, and she was very nervous. I thought to myself, "what a brave little girl." She was only eight. My own daughter, Becky, was eight, as well. I reflected upon the matter and concluded that if young Ravan was going to muster up the courage to speak, then I could...and should, too. The open microphone session was nearly at its end, and there was a long and somewhat uncomfortable pause as the microphone sat vacant and Pam contemplated bringing that segment of the program to a close. I knew it was a "now or never" moment. I took a deep breath and made my way up to the microphone.

My opening was very truthful—I told the gathered friends and family members that the story I was about to tell was one that I had been fairly certain I would take to the grave with me. Inside, I knew that if I was ever going to tell it—right here and right now was the place and time. I would tell the tale to honor my Lady Valerie. I also told the crowd that, to get through it, I would have to rely upon a few special mementos that I had brought with me.

I removed my suit jacket and boldly tossed it over to a nearby chair. I then put on a very special blue windbreaker and baseball cap.

"When I flew in last night, I wore a jacket very much like this one. But, this is not that jacket. This was the jacket I wore on a trip to Spain in 1982. And this baseball hat, while it looks like the one I was wearing the other night, is also from that same trip to Spain." As I wore those two special pieces of armor that had traveled with me to Portugal, Spain, and Morocco in 1982, I felt an amazing spirit welling up inside of me. I was ready to speak. I was finally ready to tell my story! And tell my story I did. I began at the beginning, describing highlights from the trip to Spain and how Valerie had won my heart. I interspersed a number of humorous anecdotes to keep it upbeat and fun. I was really enjoying telling the tale. My confidence grew with each moment and with each positive bit of feedback from the gathered audience. I tracked from Spain through to my long quest to finally get to British Columbia and my eventual miraculous meeting, after eight years, with my Lady. I also mentioned a few of the beautiful miracles related to Valerie and that helped to keep me inspired throughout the years. Finally, I added that I hoped that everyone would, throughout the night, share their own stories with table mates and others who had gathered—all to help keep Valerie's memory alive and honor a truly beautiful person. When I was done, I felt completely emotionally drained...but I also felt a very unique sensation of peace and relief. I felt good inside. It was a tale worth telling—a simple story of how a princess (in her tribe) saved a young man on the precipice and inspired him to be more than he ever thought he could be. When the telling was done, I knew my journey to Prince Rupert was no accident—it was full of purpose and it was meant to be. While in Prince Rupert, I made new friends and shared a special time with Valerie's friends and family. It was an incredible and enriching experience. I hoped, too, that I might have, in some way, added something to the special occasion. We all came together to share our love for a special woman who had touched us all. That's where I needed to be.

Me with Valerie's brother, Jim, and sister, Pam at the
Honour Dinner for Valerie (May 14, 2007)

The next day, feeling very much relieved, I set out for some morning Moose Hunting. I wanted to see Valerie's old house, for starters. On my Moose Hunt, I pulled out a very special note. Scribbled on a small piece of notebook paper, written during the

August 1982 visit to the New York City Public Library with my brother, was a number of addresses, including 616 Taylor. I had written Valerie's address down in 1982, and now I would finally have an opportunity to visit. While the house, sadly, had deteriorated some over the years, it was still an exhilarating experience to be there, to see the home, to see the surrounding areas, and to imagine Valerie walking those streets and living there in her younger days. The visit exemplified the true essence of a Moose Hunt.

Photo of Valerie's old home, taken during my 2007 visit

Later in the day, I went with Pam, Dave, and Joan to tour around some of the special places in town. I was in awe. I was also making mental notes—each place would earn multiple revisits by a questing knight in days (and years) to come. We met up with some additional family members in the late afternoon and were, later that evening, treated to dinner by Ruth Dudoward. The entire family was absolutely wonderful and welcomed me into their world with open arms. Their warmth really added a special touch to the trip that I have never forgotten. In fact, I often felt like, after my speech, the Dudoward family more or less adopted me. It was a beautiful feeling.

On Wednesday, May 16th, I awoke early in the morning and went out for a pleasant walk in the rain. I understand it rains a lot in Prince Rupert, and I was not about to be deterred. I sang several sea shanties in the mist. While out and about, I noticed a huge cruise ship pull up right near our hotel. I had this image of thousands of tourists flocking to the gift stores, so I thought I had better hurry and do my own shopping. I knew that if I wanted any keepsakes to take home, beyond what remained after the hoard had ravaged the local shops, I had best expedite my plans. I stumbled upon a little display of "Spirit Stones" which caught my eye. These were inspired by native petroglyphic art. At first, I thought it was a little bit gimmicky; but then I reconsidered when I noticed a moose stone. A card next to the stone described the seventeen different animals and what they symbolized. The Moose, so it said, was a "Messenger." This really struck a chord with me. I had never fully understood the reason why the moose had become such a symbol in my life—a sign. As I held that stone in the palm of my hand and pondered "the messenger," it all made sense to me. While I contemplated such magical things, I was also in tune with the beauty of my surroundings. Prince Rupert was breathtaking— a beautiful land where bald eagles were as common as sparrows and nobly perched atop lamp posts, dock pilings, and anyplace else that would support them. Cool and misty, "Rupert" was a land where mountains graciously met the sea, and magic filled the air. I was absorbing all of this as my mind continued lazily dreaming throughout the visit.

In the late afternoon, as the weather was deteriorating, we elected not to go out on the planned boat ride we had been discussing. Instead, we visited the North Pacific Cannery where Ruth had spent six years working. She made an outstanding tour guide, and I absolutely loved listening to all of her stories. She darted about the canning equipment with a flash in her eye and vividly described her time there along with other stories. I was absolutely awed by Ruth. What a terrific lady!

After a little more driving about, we returned to the hotel and, eventually, met up for dinner again. But, just before heading out for dinner, I witnessed an absolutely beautiful rainbow from my hotel window. I took a mental photo and cataloged it with the growing volume of magical Prince Rupert moments.

That evening, complements of the Dudowards, a small group of us had our final farewell dinner together at the Stardust Chinese Restaurant. After dinner, Pam and I chatted for a while; she left me with a few very nice parting gifts including a book that included poems written by Valerie and herself. It was a very special present.

The next morning, after a brief visit to Totem Hill, Pam dropped me off at the Highliner for my bus ride back to the airport. Pam actually followed the bus for a ways, as we pulled out, as a kind of final send-off. That very thoughtful escort punctuated what had been an absolutely incredible journey.

Totem pole at Totem Park, Prince Rupert (May 17, 2007)

When I finally returned to Colorado Springs, I wanted to tell

Lisa about all the events and all the wonderful people I had met, but I knew it wouldn't make sense without knowing the story behind it all. So, for the first time ever, I told my own wife the story —it was only my second telling but it was an important one. She could never know me unless she knew that story. She listened intently and did not pass judgment. In fact, she told me she was thankful for me sharing the story and that she was, likewise, glad that I was able to go on this journey to Prince Rupert to honor Valerie. I felt a wonderful sense of relief...and peace. All was right with the world.

Chapter Sixteen

A SECOND FAMILY AND MORE ADVENTURES

*A*fter Prince Rupert, my thoughts were even more focused on Valerie. It took several days before I could concentrate at work, but I eventually stabilized and returned to something resembling a daily routine. Small miracles continued to inspire me and were frequently noted in the pages of my diary—little happenings and songs popping on the radio at just the right moment. It all added up. It all made sense.

August of 2007 was special for many reasons. There was an added sadness that year because it was the first August since Valerie's passing, but it was also the 25th anniversary of my trip to Spain in 1982. I elected to read *Don Quixote* again to honor the anniversary. For five days in a row, songs I associated with 1982 came on the radio while I was listening—songs that I had not heard in ages. The anniversary was clearly shaping up as something special. On August 17th, I decided to, once more, conduct an all-night vigil to honor Valerie and the Cause. With my increasing age, I knew this would be quite difficult, but I also felt it was something I needed to do. It had been too long. I spent the night alone with my thoughts and with *Don Quixote* and my old diary volumes. Like in the past, it was a night to remember. And, like in the past, it took my body a few days to recover from the night without sleep. It was worth it!

More of those small miracles continued to fill the month until it finally ended. August 2007 was a very powerful month and one for the record books. I was truly at my best and inspiration was filling my heart.

That fall, my boss, Brigadier General Susan Desjardins, informed me that she was giving me command of a Cadet Group in the spring and that I would be commanding Basic Cadet Training that summer. I knew this meant a lot of work, but I was very excited and very grateful to General Desjardins for affording me these incredible opportunities. Cadet Group 2 was comprised of over 1,100 cadets; during Basic Cadet Training, I would command over 2,400 cadets and permanent party members. This was big stuff. We were shaping the development of the next generation of Air Force officers, and it was imperative that we got it right.

In the fall of 2007, I was invited, once again, to head up to Prince Rupert, Canada. This time, the Dudoward family was hosting a First Nations Feast and Naming Ceremony. I definitely wanted to be a part of that event and wasted no time in making preparations for the travel.

I departed for Prince Rupert on November 9, 2007. Ruth and Pam Dudoward had rented a house in Prince Rupert since they were planning on staying up there for an extended period of time. They insisted I stay with them at no cost. I felt very honored for the trust; and of course, the free lodging was an added bonus. Again, they made me feel very much like part of the Dudoward family. I had the whole bottom floor of the house to myself. It was great! The view from the upstairs balcony was nothing short of breathtaking. I spent each morning eating toast and jam with Ruth. Pam is a night owl and tended to sleep in so, during the morning hours, I got to enjoy wonderful stories of Tsimshian culture and traditions, as only Ruth could tell them. I really loved this time with Ruth Dudoward. She was truly a remarkable and wise woman—I could have listened to her stories forever.

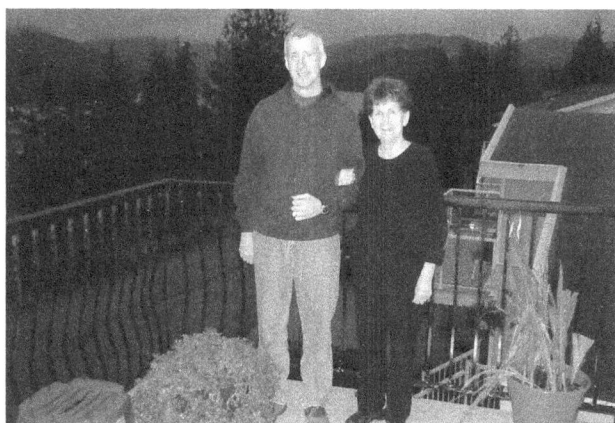

Me and Ruth Dudoward (November, 2007)

The Feast itself, on November 10th, was quite a remarkable experience. The event began at 4:00 pm and was filled with rich traditions, pride, humor, and great camaraderie. Five Chiefs attended the event and several spoke. The meal was simple but very good—soup and homemade rolls, cake, and fruit. Dancers and traditional drummers helped to create a special atmosphere and made the event a timeless gathering. The highlight of the evening, for me, was getting to see Pam and Jim Dudoward receive their names and Ruth get her name strengthened. I was honored to be part of it all and share in the laughter, the pride, and a few tears, as well. On the morning of my departure, November 13th, I managed to talk Pam into driving me around a little bit to do some last-minute Moose Hunting. We visited several sites where Valerie had lived and the Civic Center where she won the Miss Prince Rupert contest back in 1974. We also got to visit Valerie's old high school where there was actually a photo of Valerie and her class-mates hanging in the hallway. That was very special. Finally, it was time for me to head home. Once again, I said a fond farewell to Prince Rupert, hoping I would get to return again someday. Once again, the journey had been a very special one for me.

Upon my return to Colorado, thoughts of Valerie flooded my head. If I may illustrate, I will share my diary entry from November 18, 2007. This was written several days after my return:

Weekend comes to a close and so too my very pleasant time off. Valerie has really been on my mind a lot the last few days—very strong feelings in my heart. I miss her so and I am so sad that she is gone—but she must be free to continue on her journey—I pray the angels are caring well for my Lady. What a very special person—truly beautiful. A true princess and I didn't even know it—perhaps I should have. Modest and reserved, always dignified and so gentle of spirit—a woman of quality through and through. But much beyond what words could ever express was the extraordinary feeling of peace I felt within my heart whenever she was near. So very special—she saved my life. I miss you, Valerie. Perhaps, one day, in another time and place, we shall meet again. Until then, I shall keep your memory close to my heart and we shall meet where so often we have met before—in my dreams. I look forward to our next meeting. Be well, my Lady Valerie.

November 23, 2007. I awoke feeling very blessed after an amazing Valerie dream. It had been quite some time since I'd had such a vivid and significant dream about Valerie. The dream involved both of us being on a trip abroad, but the undefined location was not Spain. Instead, it was a cool and rainy location, very reminiscent of Vancouver. In my dream, much as during my trip to Spain, I was desperately trying to spend time with Valerie, but she was quite elusive. And, like in Spain, everybody really liked her and wanted to spend time with her. One funny part of the dream involved a dining room where we ate all our meals. They moved the tour group to a larger dining room with larger rectangular tables. With the larger tables, there was one free space at the table I was sitting at and everyone was insisting that the open chair should be placed next to them and reserved for Valerie. I finally won out and the open chair for Valerie was placed right next to me...and we did have several meals together. As dreams often have surrealistic parts, so too did this one. In this dream, Valerie was also working part-time in a little gift shop at our hotel that sold T-shirts and baseball caps. I would often walk by the shop to see if she was in. Most of the time, she was not. But, sometimes, I would get lucky. At the very end of the dream, I got moved to another room where the night table was completely filled with bags of pretzels and other snack foods. Don't even ask me the significance. I don't know. In the dream, my parents were also on the trip but they made only a brief appearance in the story. They told me that they were going to have to depart the tour a few days early and head home. I was panicking that I wouldn't be able to say farewell to Valerie before our departure, and I scrambled to arrange a final meeting so that I could say a better farewell than I had been able to say in Spain. Valerie dropped by my room, after my pleading, and we spent quite a bit of time talking together. I told her how much she meant to me and how important she had been in my life. Later, in the cool and cloudy morning, we went out for a walk together. The dream walk was filled with powerful messages that I would consider long after I woke up. Valerie was being incredibly warm and kind, yet she was also trying to be careful so that I would not become too attached and fall in love which she knew might result in a dysfunctional life were I to forsake all other relationships to hold on to my love for her. Finally, after considering, she gave me a big hug and a kiss on the cheek and said farewell. It was very special and warm. I went back to my room in a dreamy state and packed my bags to go, sad that I would be leaving Valerie. At this point, I awoke from my dream, at around 4:00 am. I woke feeling very good inside and immediately grabbed some paper to write about my dream, lest I forget it with time. It felt so very wonderful to have such a vivid and complete Valerie dream again. Surely, the dream had meaning and deep significance. Beyond that, it was lovely to see Valerie, young and energetic, just as she had been in Spain. It was beautiful.

Valentine's Day. I have purposefully not been noting all the numerous times that songs came on the radio at special moments because my diary is filled with such marvelous "coincidences," but I did want to note another special Valentine's Day message. On February 14, 2008, I got off work late and decided that I would pick up some Chinese food on the way home. The food took longer than I was expecting to prepare as the restaurant was very busy. While the late night in the office might have been frustrating, as was the delay in getting my food, both set the stage for a rather nice Valentine's gift. As I left the Chinese restaurant for the short five-minute drive home, I turned on my car radio, knowing I'd only have time for one song. Just as I turned on the radio, the announcer said that the next song would be a Steve Winwood song. Sure enough, it was "Valerie." I was smiling all the way home. This was truly another special blessing. And on Valentine's Day, I remembered she who had captured my heart back in 1982, my Lady Valerie.

The year progressed and I eventually surged into the summer where regular 2:00 am wake up alarms for Basic Training truly tested my endurance. Still, the thrill of running the Academy's largest summer program and the excitement of command kept me going through the exhaustion.

Leading the Basic Cadet Training formation on the march to Jacks Valley, United States Air Force Academy

Eventually, we entered into the Academic year; I established a lengthy but much more reasonable work schedule. The signs continued and bolstered my spirit when I most needed it. On September 7, 2008, the anniversary of when I finally got to see Valerie again, I was in my home office and decided to turn on the radio—a radio I had not listened to in months. Just as I turned it on, "Ramble On" began to play. How could I ever doubt?!

Work continued to be very challenging and was filled with long days. In May 2009, I had another welcome break for a very special event. Years ago, in fact, not long after her return from Spain, Valerie had written a marvelous play, *Teach Me the Ways of the Sacred Circle*. It had originally been produced on stage back in 1986, but Pam Dudoward wanted to bring the play to life again and had gone to great lengths to set up a Vancouver production for the play to help raise money for the Valerie Dudoward Foundation, a charity established in Valerie's name to provide support to aboriginal youth and women who had suffered abusive relationships and were in need of help. While I was in Vancouver, in an unprecedented display of trust and caring, Ruth Dudoward insisted I not pay for a hotel but that I stay in the guest bedroom of her apartment. I hardly knew what to say. Outside of my own family, I had rarely seen this kind of kindness. The giving spirit of Ruth Dudoward was undeniable. When I ponder human nature, it's the Ruth Dudowards of the world that I look to for restoring my faith in the goodness within the human heart. One person can make a difference in this world. Ruth Dudoward, much like her daughter, was such a person.

At the play, I participated in an opening segment on stage to draw attention to the pervasiveness of domestic abuse. I was a little nervous to get up on stage, but the cause was worthy and I was glad to be part of the evening. The play was absolutely wonderful—it's a beautiful commentary on the tension faced by aboriginal youth in an urban environment as they attempt to blend into a modern society while simultaneously attempting to embrace their own unique and beautiful culture. I really loved the play. I was so proud of Pam for all the work she had done to pull it all together. After the play, there were poetry readings of Valerie's work and also a beautiful video production with photos from Valerie's life. The first night of the production was on May 16th. The second evening was to hold its own special magic.

Vancouver production of Valerie's play, "Teach Me the Ways of the Sacred Circle" (May 16, 2009)

Prior to the night of the first production, I had to think about which coat I wanted to wear to the play. I finally elected not to wear my windbreaker and opted for a heavier coat with a greater abundance of much-needed pockets that I knew I would need. I was hardly in the cab before I started doubting my decision. I had this hard-to-explain feeling that I had chosen poorly. All the same, the night went well.

Prior to the showing on May 17th, I sought to remedy my error from the first night. If Valerie was looking down upon us all from Heaven, I wanted her to know, without doubt, that her knight was there to pay homage to his lady. I wore my blue windbreaker and baseball cap—both of the same style that I had worn in Spain in 1982 and again in Vancouver in 1990.

We all arrived at the theater together and, while waiting for things to start up, I grabbed a seat on one of the theater benches. In the background, the theater's public-address system was playing music while patrons enjoyed food and perused the donated items for sale to support the Valerie Dudoward Foundation. As I sat there, I was completely awestruck when a very familiar song came across the speakers—it was Led Zeppelin's "Ramble On!" I asked around later to make sure no one had a hand in this happening—I was the only one who even noticed it. This song, of course, was the song I most associated with my questing and dream of one day finding Valerie again. That this song should come on a theater speaker system on this particular occasion was nothing short of a miracle. I had no doubt it was a sign from Valerie. I felt an immediate sense of comfort. I felt that Valerie knew I was there and this was her way of saying thank you for me coming to her play. I was glad I had chosen to wear my armor—I knew Valerie would recognize me in the windbreaker and cap. My heart was so filled with joy and love! I felt an ethereal lightness throughout the remainder of the evening. The second night of the play was no less spectacular than the first and, with the added miracle, it was a day I shall never forget. I believe!

I remained in Vancouver for several days after the play and the miracles kept coming. On May 19th, I went for another long walk along the Sea Wall. As my throat was getting a little bit scratchy, I decided to stop by Whole Foods to get some throat lozenges. Just as I exited the store and was standing in the midst of a spectacular floral display, the song "You're Beautiful" came on over the store's PA system. I was stopped in my tracks and listened to the entire song as I knew it was special to Valerie...and to me. That afternoon, Pam and I drove all over Vancouver looking at the places they used to live. I took lots of photos and felt completely at peace on that special Moose Hunting excursion. We also visited the cemetery where a marker was placed in Valerie's honor next to her father's grave. Prior to visiting, I purchased a very large bouquet of purple flowers to lay at the site. Purple was Valerie's favorite color and, interestingly enough, the color I most associated with Valerie through the years. I placed the flowers by Valerie's marker, and Pam placed some flowers at her father's grave. Eventually, Pam returned to the vehicle to allow me some time alone at the spot. I spent quite a while sitting there. It was very emotional for me. Finally, I placed a kiss upon Valerie's marker before returning to the vehicle for a silent return trip.

The next day was filled with more Moose Hunting. This time, I retraced some of my steps from my 1990 visit to Vancouver, that being the time I was finally reunited with Valerie. I returned to Stanley Park and the Aquarium. I wandered all through the park and did lots of thinking. I then strayed into the downtown area for a visit I knew would be very difficult. I walked to Robson Street and then retraced my steps to Shenanigans where Valerie and I met. I stepped inside and spent some time at the spot where we sat and talked for several hours on that magical 7th day of September 1990. I finally left Shenanigans and walked to the spot from which I had my last view of Valerie—she looking back at me with caring eyes. I stood and looked across the pavement to where I saw her last. It was a very poignant visit. After a deep sigh, I turned and continued on my walk. I had no direction in mind—I just knew I needed to walk that off. After straying deeper into the downtown area, I finally headed for a bus stop and a return trip towards Ruth's apartment. Ruth made a wonderful dinner that night and we talked for hours. A day that had begun with stomach problems ended with great meaning and inspiration—like so many Moose Hunts before.

Revisiting Shenanigans on Robson, Vancouver (May
20, 2009)

I returned from Vancouver a few days later, but part of the
magic followed me home. In this instance, I think my diary tells
the story best. Taken from my diary entry on May 23, 2009:

*Amazing! Amazing and Wonderful! It's hard to write, I'm so excited.
Thank you, Valerie! I know you are still with us—I have no doubt.*

*As part of the Valerie DVD presentation, there was this one photo
that really caught my eye—a photo of Valerie riding a camel. I asked
Pam about it and she told me it was Valerie from a trip to Turkey. Her*

hair looked very much as I remembered it from our trip. Valerie looked very much as I remembered her from our trip. I asked Pam if I could get a copy of that photo sometime. I was interested in a few other photos, too; but Pam simply ran out of time with all she had going on. However, as a parting gift, she gave me a copy of that photo in a frame. Something still looked strangely familiar about the scene, but Pam was sure the photo was from a different trip. Well, just a few moments ago I was looking at this wonderful photo when, for the first time, I noticed something totally amazing. I've always looked at Valerie on the camel, but now I noticed she was not alone in the scene —a young man in a blue windbreaker, blue and white baseball cap, Addidas sneakers, and blue jeans, looks on from the right side of the frame—IT'S ME!

Totally amazing—thank you!!! 27 years later—a photo from what I now know is Morocco with Valerie and I together—forever. It's hard to describe the joy in my heart. Valerie keeps giving, though her soul and spirit now journey through unknown lands. Your knight rides with you, my lady; and my love remains, as before, undying. Bless you always, my dearest Lady Valerie—I love you. I love you. I love you!

The significance of that special gift cannot be overstated. For so many years, I had a crazy dream that somewhere, somehow, one of the tourists on our trip might have a photo where both Valerie and I were captured in time...together. It was just a dream. I never thought to see any of these people again, much less have them dig out a photo from a quarter-century before that would match the dream. And then, a gift from Heaven. I cannot help but think upon all this with a sense of wonder and awe. The world is a beautiful place and miracles are real. Very real.

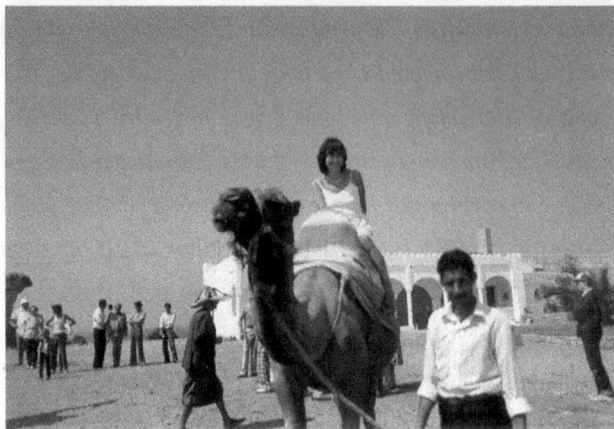

Photo of Valerie on a camel, Morocco (August 7, 1982)

About a month after my return from Vancouver, on Sunday, June 21, 2009, I had the opportunity to attend a wonderful concert in Denver. It was actually the first Rock Concert I ever attended, and the artists were none other than Steve Winwood and Eric Clapton. It was awesome! Steve Winwood is an artist whose music I've always loved. Several of his works have direct associations with Valerie and 1982. The most significant, of course, is the song "Valerie," which he released in 1982. It naturally had lots of radio play, in those days, and always reminded me of my Lady Valerie. Several other songs also had special ties. One of my all-time favorite songs, "Dear Mr. Fantasy," is a song I always associate with my daydreaming extravaganzas in 1982. I was absolutely thrilled when Steve Winwood sang it as an encore for the concert. I was on my feet and singing along. The very next day, I was notified by the Vice Commandant that I had been selected for promotion to the rank of Colonel. It was a good week.

At work, things continued to be stressful and busy. At home, I was still riding the high from recent events; and I tried to carry some of that motivation with me into another celebratory August.

Once again, besides just focusing on my own August agenda, I tried to make the month a special one for the kids by creating an on-going adventure story complete with stuffed animal heroes, props, and wonderment. We all had fun.

On January 22, 2010, I had my promotion ceremony. This was the last duty day before the date my new rank became official, February 1, 2010. The ceremony was held at Arnold Hall which seemed very appropriate—it was here that I was first sworn in as a cadet in the United States Air Force back on July 6, 1984. I was fairly certain Colonel would be my final rank—hence the symmetry. I like bookends. The ceremony went very well. It was a memorable day. I purposefully held the ceremony a little bit early so that I could take some leave to go skiing with Tommy. We usually went skiing in February, but I had crafted some spectacularly huge plans for the coming month—plans that would unite several powerful themes in my life.

For years, I had been wrestling with a rather interesting prospect. While I knew it would be cost-prohibitive, when I found out that the 2010 Winter Olympics would be held in Vancouver, British Columbia, I saw a unique convergence of two very special parts of my life. Ever since I first saw Dorothy Hamill skate to Olympic Gold in Innsbruck in 1976, I had been a huge fan of the winter games and of figure skating, in general. The significance of the city of Vancouver should, by now, be abundantly clear. I knew this convergence was unlikely to happen again anytime soon...and perhaps never again in my lifetime. Finally, after much hand wringing, I convinced myself that the spiritual journey was worth the financial cost. Still, with some notion of sanity remaining in the plan, I elected to only visit for the second half of the games. This scaled-back adventure, alone, would cost me over $10,000. It was a daunting prospect—but I was willing to depart with the money to fulfill a dream. While I would have loved to take my family, the $60,000 price tag was well outside my financial limits.

The Olympics officially began on February 12th, which happens to be a special anniversary date for me, in and of itself. I watched the first week on television from home. On February 21st, I was there in person. While I had purchased tickets for several events, my major goal was to get tickets for both the Ladies Short Program and the Free Skate. Although it cost me, and I had to make it happen by purchasing a rather pricey hotel package deal, I was ultimately successful in realizing this dream.

While I was in Vancouver, my travels took me not only to Olympic venues but also on several Moose Hunting adventures. I visited briefly with Pam Dudoward who, while protecting Valerie's journal with her life, was kind enough to let me read a small section that recounted part of our shared trip to Spain in 1982.

Standing beside the Olympic flame, Vancouver (February, 2010)

As I read Valerie's words, memories came flooding back. It was a very powerful experience, and I am grateful to Pam for sharing Valerie's words with me and for protecting the rest of the journal with the ferocity of a lioness protecting her cubs.

My Olympic experience was an amazingly wonderful one. There were trials and complications and many of the elements that have made for good stories throughout my life. When all was said and done, I did get to enjoy the beauty and powerful magnificence of the skating events I had so longed to see. But this was not all. Amidst the Olympic fanfare, Vancouver had yet one more blessing to bestow upon me—a final sign.

Women's Olympic Figure Skating medal ceremony
(February 25, 2010)

February 27, 2010. The day did not start out well. It was to start with a routine visit to the train station I had used several times before, followed by a bus trip up to Whistler to see the final runs of the four-man bobsled. I woke with some pretty bad diarrhea but was unwilling to cancel my plans. I took some more anti-diarrheal medication and, at 6:30 am, headed out into the pouring rain. I got completely soaked in the cold rain—it did not feel good. As I headed towards the train station, something very strange happened. Somehow, although I had made the trip successfully a number of times before, I got lost. Maybe it's because I was sick, or because it was dark and raining? I don't know. Somewhere, I made a wrong turn; I was lost in Vancouver. All I had to do was head down Nelson Street, hang a left on Granville, and head to the station. But that's not where my legs carried me. To this date, I don't know how I got turned around. After wandering for a while, in a daze, trying to pick up something that looked familiar, I decided to take shelter under an overhanging canopy and look at my map. The rain was still coming down very heavily. And this is when I noticed something that completely blew my mind. It was nothing short of miraculous. I was standing beneath the entry awning for the Anchor Point Apartments! I then recognized this as one of the places I had visited with Pam on our "This was Valerie's Life Tour." Valerie used to live there. I stood there in complete amazement. This was a miracle! Surely, this "accident" was no accident. As I stood there, all my worries faded away. I was no longer concerned about my stomach cramps, no longer concerned about being soaking wet, and no longer worried that I might miss my bus up to the bobsledding event. I felt only a sense of gratitude and a feeling of peace within my soul.

When all was said and done, after some more travel chaos and misdirection, I did catch my bus, only minutes before it departed. I was very chilled during the two-hour bus ride up to Whistler. I knew I would not fare well were I to watch the three-hour bobsled competition, upon the top of the mountain, in my wet clothes. Despite the cost, I went into a ski shop at Whistler Village and purchased some new clothes to wear. I can still remember the funny look they gave me at the security checkpoint when I handed them a bag filled with wet clothing. I was dry, and I enjoyed the bobsledding. Better yet, U.S.A. Team One, piloted by Steve Holcomb, took the Olympic gold that day. It all added up to another unforgettable life experience for me.

The next day, I attended the closing ceremonies and ended my special adventure.

Back in "the real world," we quickly approached the end of our tour in Colorado. After refinancing our house, we put it on the market in hopes of getting a renter. If we had tried to sell the property, in the aftermath of the 2008 housing market crash, we would have been looking at something like an $80,000 loss. This was not a financially viable course of action for us. Even amidst the mounting stress of the move and our financial situation, I continued to compartmentalize my spiritual life, keeping it distinct and separate from the day-to-day challenges that life posed. I knew that I could not permit my daily hardships to wear away at my faith.

On Memorial Day weekend, we hit the road for my next assignment to Barksdale Air Force Base, Louisiana. I was hired to be the Chief of the Combat Plans Division in the 608th Air and Space Operations Center. I had barely in-processed at the base when I was sent TDY, down to Hurlburt Air Base, Florida, to attend a training course to help prepare me for my current duties. Meanwhile, in Louisiana, with no housing available in the local area, we were stuck living in a single-wide trailer on the edge of a bayou (literally about ten to fifteen feet from the edge) with alligators as our neighbors. This was quite a welcome to Louisiana. The "Fam Camp" trailer would be our home for the next three months.

Our single-wide FEMA trailer home, Barksdale Air Force Base, LA
(2010)

While my life was very busy and chaotic, Pam Dudoward was likewise fully engaged up in Canada dealing with a myriad of issues related to the upcoming production of *Teach Me...* in Prince Rupert. Things were not simple, and it seemed Pam was running into walls at every turn. Still, she pressed on. Attending this play was the next big agenda item on my adventure calendar.

Certain aspects of my personal and professional life felt like they were starting to crumble, and I was losing the ability to repair them. It was a very difficult time for me. I did the only thing I knew how to do—I drew even closer to the spiritual side of me that had given me strength throughout the years. I eagerly looked forward to my journey to Prince Rupert. On July 15, 2010, I was headed north again. After another very long day of travel, I finally found myself back in the magical, and very familiar, little town that Valerie had called home. I noted in my diary that, on the flight up, I decided to peruse a magazine I found in the seatback in front of me. It just so happened that this magazine was written entirely in Spanish. Within its pages was a picture of Don Quixote and Sancho Panza. I smiled a knowing smile. I was re-entering my world. This was a trip I was meant to take. I purchased another copy of *Don Quixote* at the airport in Vancouver. I already owned several editions of the novel, but it seemed appropriate to have one purchased in that magical city. After the layover at the Vancouver International Airport, I was once more on my way up to Prince Rupert.

On the morning of July 16th, I departed early on a Moose Hunting excursion that led me to many sites of significance. I walked for miles, and my mind wandered the corridors of inspiration freely. Positive thoughts filled my head as I journeyed, and peace filled my heart. I returned after approximately four hours, had lunch, and then did some reading in my hotel room at the Inn on the Harbour. Shortly after 3:30 pm, I began my walk to the Lester Art Centre for the first day's production of *Teach Me the Ways of the Sacred Circle*. While there, I got to speak with several friends I had made on previous visits, as I waited for the 6:00 pm showtime. Once again, I volunteered to be a "clapper" up on stage, prior to the start of the play, as part of the introductory piece highlighting the frequency of domestic abuse episodes in Canada. Again, I was proud to be part of the production.

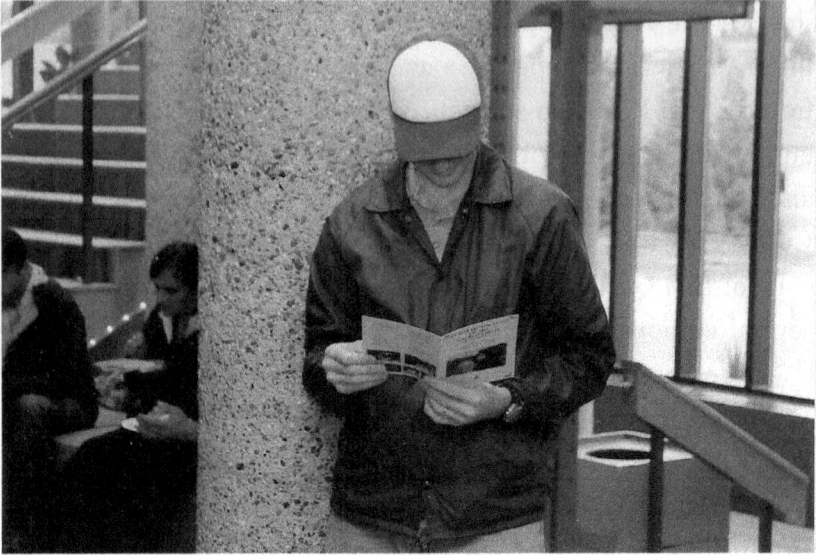

Reviewing the play program before the Prince Rupert production of
"Teach Me the Ways of the Sacred Circle" at the Lester Arts Centre
(July 16, 2010)

A number of Valerie's poems were read, and then the play began. Once again, I thought the actors did a fine job of recreating Valerie's vision upon the stage. Most of the actors were First Nations, which was only appropriate. I was so glad to be able to see the premiere of Valerie's play in her own hometown. That had great meaning for me. The evening concluded, again, with a video presentation of Valerie's life, along with some other family photos.

July 17th began much like the day before—more Moose Hunting in Prince Rupert. On my morning Moose Hunting trek, I stumbled upon a postcard just laying in the grass along my route. I picked it up and looked at it. It was a postcard of a castle. I had to smile. In this instance, I carefully replaced the postcard where I found it. Left in place, I thought perhaps it might inspire yet another knight errant upon his lonely journey. During my Moose Hunting journeys, I have frequently been blessed by such welcome signs. On this outing, I purchased a Killer Whale Loyalty Coin at the Museum of Northern British Columbia. As Valerie was of the Tsimshian Killer Whale Clan, the "Loyalty" coin seemed incredibly appropriate. I had much to give thanks for, and loyalty was always an attribute I found in great abundance within my heart.

I returned to my room, bounced my green rubber ball (the same one that came with me to Spain) in the room for a while, and waited until it was time to go to the play.

My final day in Prince Rupert, July 18th, was spent much as the days before. I was out and about enjoying the beauty of the city while visiting numerous Moose Hunting sites and dreaming away the hours of the day. While not actively Moose Hunting, I was daydreaming down by the water's edge. A killer whale watching tour I had scheduled for late in the day wound up canceling when they failed to get the required number of passengers signed up to make the excursion financially viable. I was somewhat disappointed, but I didn't let the cancellation dampen my enthusiasm. I elected to dine alone at the Stardust Chinese Restaurant, a Dudoward family favorite. The day had already been special. Not only had I enjoyed hours of Moose Hunting adventures, but I also stumbled upon a very appropriate show on television—it was a show about knights. Even as I ate my final meal in the town, Prince Rupert was conjuring one final, special parting gift for me.

After finishing my meal at Stardust, I went to wash my hands in the restroom. When I returned, a fortune cookie was sitting at my place. This was interesting. I was expecting to get another cheesy fortune, as is often the case. What I received was a lovely and special message. The fortune within my cookie said simply, "Someone special admires you." Perfect. I could only hope and pray that that "someone special" was Valerie. It was a perfect way to end my visit to Prince Rupert. I was not sure if I would ever get back again. I socialized very little during the trip, but I truly felt like Valerie was with me. I wore some of the same clothes I had worn in 1982 (which, incredibly, still fit). Better yet, I could still feel the magic all about. The temperatures had been between fifty-five and sixty degrees Fahrenheit, perfect windbreaker weather; I never once got rained upon—a rarity for Prince Rupert. Once again, my trip across the Canadian border turned into a beautifully inspirational journey for my soul.

Not long after my return to Louisiana, during the night of 26 to 27 July, I had an incredible night of dreams with both a Valerie and Dorothy dream on the same night. That had never happened before. It is interesting to note that July 26th is Dorothy's birthday. The dreams were both amazingly vivid. In the Valerie dream, Val was there, very much alive, and wearing the purple outfit from Spain that was my favorite. The dream was very comforting. In it, Valerie assured me that she was alive and okay. While she appeared to be in her mid-twenties, as she was in Spain, the dream was not in any way historical. During this dream, I was struggling with her loss—and then Valerie appeared—she immediately put me at ease, as she was so good at doing. Valerie continued to assure me that she was alive. And I believed. I still do. I know her beautiful soul lives on!

The Dorothy dream segment was not quite as emotional, but it was also significant in its own way. During the dream, I was trying to get to Madison Square Garden to see Dorothy skate; but I got lost on the subway and ended up in a strange part of the city. I tried to find a train back but could not. I finally lucked into hailing down a cab and made it to the show only moments before it started. This was very reminiscent of my Ladies' Figure Skating Short Program experience during the Olympics, earlier in the year. However, in my dream, I was given a front-row seat to see

Dorothy skate. I felt very fortunate. At this point in the dream, I woke up. When I awoke, I had a sense of renewed dedication and purpose. Such signs are never to be taken lightly. They all have meaning and they are always a call to fortify one's faith. It was a blessing to spend the night with my ladies.

Chapter Seventeen

A FINAL FAREWELL

August of 2010 certainly came with some logistical challenges. Crammed within the confines of our single-wide trailer, it was difficult to honor the month in the ways I was accustomed to. While lacking from a ceremonial perspective, I did my best to ensure that the month was not short on reflection or faith.

In September, we finally found an off-base house that we could rent. Our new home was a somewhat run-down country house which was clearly over-priced. With that said, we were all very happy just to escape from the trailer. Those trailers were not meant to house six people and a large dog. Despite that fact, we all had a warm spot in our hearts for that old trailer—after all, it was our lifeboat for three months. When our household goods were finally delivered to the new home, I was saddened to see the shattered remains of my entire wooden ship model fleet. My beautiful ships were completely destroyed during the move. There was quite a bit of other damage, too; but the loss of my ships was very painful. I had guarded them for many years, usually moving them myself. Since I knew we would have no house to move into, I had to trust them to the military's choice of moving companies. Clearly, they chose poorly; my fleet suffered the consequences. Things like that, however, allow you to reflect on what is truly important in life. In the end, things could have been much worse. People matter, not possessions.

At work, things continued pretty much as normal until our unanticipated involvement in Operation Odyssey Dawn. With little notice, we were called upon to develop long-range Global Strike bomber options to support the United Nations Security Council Resolution designed to protect Libyan citizens during the Libyan Civil War. With the situation getting more perilous, the international community deemed it was time to act. In the 608th Air and Space Operations Center, we scrambled to put together a plan. Though the days were long, I felt very proud to lead the planning effort to make these short-notice Global Strike missions a reality. When all was said and done, the missions we planned with our small team resulted in the destruction of 17% of the targets eliminated during that operation. These missions also represented a number of "firsts" to include the first-ever Global Strike missions flown by B-1 bombers from the Continental United States (CONUS) and the first-ever Global Strike missions flown by United States Strategic Command. I am confident that our work saved countless innocent lives. Operations such as these helped to remind me of the importance of our mission.

June 11, 2011. All morning and the night before, an old Doors song kept running through my head as I thought upon Valerie, knights, and related things. The song was "Touch Me." One line, especially, kept running through my brain: "I'm going to love you, 'til the heavens stop the rain, I'm going to love you 'til the stars fall from the sky for you and I." The line kept playing over and over in my head. Later in the day, as I drove home from a change of command ceremony, "Touch Me" came on the radio—it was the first time I had heard the song in Louisiana. I just smiled and looked up to the heavens...then quickly back to the road.

August 2011 came and I celebrated...but perhaps not as much as I should have. My diary entries were frighteningly sparse that year. I received some shocking news in September that recalibrated my mental state. Valerie's Mom, dear Ruth Dudoward, had suffered a stroke; she was not doing well at all. As if this wasn't bad enough news, a few short months later, I received word that my brother's wife had passed away. While technically still married, my brother and his wife, Olivia, had been living separately for many years. Olivia had a congenital heart condition, and we believe that was the cause of her death. It was a very sad time, for sure. My heart went out to my brother—I knew he was really suffering.

With all the sadness abounding, my Friends from above remained there to comfort me. Allow me to share my diary entry from December 24, 2011, to help illustrate what I mean.

Christmas Eve. Too long now have I been lacking passion, and I hate to be without a mission or quest. Things seem better today, and I feel some magic in the air—I can't really explain the how or why of it, but I feel it, truly. The night before last, Lisa said I was talking in my sleep and blurted out "Where am I!?" When I went to bed last night, that theme was on my mind, and I dreamt of asking an angel that question. I dreamt I was in total darkness—no sight, sound, or feeling. In my dream, I shouted "Where am I!?" (much as Lisa said I did the previous night). But in my dreams, my angel spoke softly to comfort me (the first sound to my ears), and she held my hand (my first feeling), and then I saw her beautiful face, illuminated through the darkness. Slowly, I saw stars begin to populate the sky and I heard waves gently washing ashore and I felt the soft sand below. My angel and I were laying on an isolated stretch of beach holding hands and gazing up at the stars—it was beautiful and I felt at peace. I was very much at peace. A good night. I woke this morning feeling like I was not alone. I felt magic in the air and, for the first time in months, I drew the sword and I felt whole again. A very good day, this day before Christmas. Dream. Believe. Live!"

On December 27, 2011, I received some very bad news...news I had been dreading. Ruth Dudoward passed away. She had been ill for so long. Ruth had been like a second mother to me. It was a great loss. My only consolation was a firm belief that she was finally at peace and finally reunited with Valerie and Jim Dudoward, Senior, in Heaven.

The loss of Ruth Dudoward would draw me back to Prince Rupert one more time. Pam was setting up an Honour Dinner for her mother in May, and I knew I had to be there. I arrived in Prince Rupert on May 10th after another long journey that included a very reflective layover in Vancouver. Pam Dudoward arranged for me and several other close friends to stay with her at the Eagle Bluff Bed and Breakfast. This B&B literally backed up to the dock; the view from my window upon the bay and mountains beyond was wonderfully breathtaking. I watched eagles land to greet the arriving fishing vessels and saw harbor seals pop up, only a short way off, to survey the scene. It was all very beautiful.

With a friend, Prince Rupert, B.C., Canada (May, 2012)

The first few days in Prince Rupert were filled with small gatherings and preparations for Sunday's Honour Dinner. Naturally, I spent many hours each day wandering around Prince Rupert, a city which by now was very familiar to me. As I enjoyed myself along the dockside, I could see eagles flying everywhere. It was unbelievable! In one instance, a beautiful bald eagle flew directly over me, only a few feet above my head. This was Heaven for an animal lover like me.

On Sunday afternoon, I helped set up for the Honour Dinner at Chances. The event kicked off just after 4:00 pm with First Nations drummers, beautiful tribute speeches, and a lovely photo slideshow presentation. There was also an open microphone session, but I elected not to speak at this event. There were plenty of friends and family members who all had beautiful things to say. It was a lovely gathering and a fitting tribute to a beautiful woman.

If Sunday, the 13th, had been an emotional day to honor a special woman, then Monday, the 14th, was no less. Pam had something very special planned for the day. She had arranged, through family, to charter a cruise on a local fishing vessel. Amazingly (but perhaps not coincidentally), this day was the one non-rainy and absolutely clear day of the entire trip. It was a perfect day. Windbreaker and baseball cap on, I boarded the fishing vessel and felt immediately at home as we got underway. I even climbed up, up, up to the crow's nest, far above the deck, and admired the stunning beauty of British Columbia. What made this journey so special, however, was not the scenery or the ride—it was the destination. We were headed to the spot where Valerie's ashes had been scattered so that we might pay our respects in the way we each saw fit.

We turned off the motor, and everyone was silent as we held our station just off Tugwell. Pam brought some of Valerie's favorite candy which she tossed into the water. I tossed some, too. Then I knelt.

East Isle fishing boat (May 14, 2012)

Climbing up to the crows nest on the *East Isle* (May 14, 2012)

I held on to the side of the boat as I looked out across the waters. I was silent. The words in my heart were saying all that needed to be said. For many minutes, I kept my post. Finally, before getting to my feet again, I said the only four words I wanted to vocalize—"I love you, Valerie."

After this very quiet and meaningful pause, our vessel got underway again; the conversations eventually resumed. It had been a very magical visit to an incredibly special place, both physically and spiritually. After our return, Pam, Allyson, and I had dinner together at Breakers. It came as absolutely no surprise when not one, nor two, but three of my favorite old songs from 1982 came on the radio at the restaurant as we ate. It was magical! A gift from Heaven.

When I finally returned home from this, my last trip to Prince Rupert, and was unpacking, I was given a final gift. This gift came in the form of another sign, not unlike my final "gift" from my previous visit. I set my iPod music player up to listen to some songs while I unpacked from the journey. I set it to randomly shuffle between the over 4,000 songs on the device. The first song to be played, during this random shuffle, was Steve Winwood's "Valerie." Perfect. It was perfect. All I could do was thank God and thank my Lady Valerie who I knew had not abandoned her knight. I will never abandon her. I still harbor the hope that one day, in a far distant land, we might meet once again. It is a dream I have.

Rarely, in life, do we meet someone who has the ability to change lives in the way that Valerie changed mine. She saved my life—it's as simple as that. Valerie was brilliant, brave, caring, and so very giving. Perhaps she gave too much? She left us too soon, but the contributions she made to this world are undeniable and live on as a lasting legacy to the beauty of her soul. A little bit of Valerie lives on in each of us who owe our lives and well-being to her compassion. We must carry the torch forward and help light the way for those lost in the darkness. Lady Valerie lives! She continues to inspire me. She will always be the radiant and perfect

Dulcinea to my fumbling and unworthy Don Quixote. I shall forever seek to be worthy of the gifts she has given me.

I look back and wonder at an incredible array of miracles and life-changing events. I am grateful. I look forward to the unknown future and know only that I must be brave, and I must never forsake my faith nor give in to the temptations that lead to the destruction of our soul. I have ridden along the mist-enshrouded bank of a magical river and, occasionally, crossed the bridge to the other side. And, oh, the things I've seen! It is Valerie that I remember most. On my journey through La Mancha, I found not only my beautiful lady—I found myself.

Chapter Eighteen

A KNIGHT RIDES ON

 cross a snow-covered field, a man in armor rides. The land is quiet. Only the sound of the wind dares to disrupt this solemn silence. But for the gentle swaying of distant branches and the steamy breath emanating from his gallant charger's nostrils, the scene is perfectly still—a frozen winter wonderland.

In the distance, there's a small disturbance at the edge of the ancient forest. Bushes rustle. Branches sway. And then all is still. Tranquility is restored. The brave warrior wheels about upon his horse and heads towards where this fleeting scene played out. The knight is careful not to let the reins out. While his mount is eager, there is no need to disrupt the peaceful serenity of the day. There is time enough for all that must be accomplished. All things will happen at their appointed time and God, alone, is master of the clock.

Beneath the battered and well-worn metal that protects this warrior from physical damage is an armor of much greater value —the true shield protecting his existence through the darkness and solitude of the harsh wilderness. It's this spiritual armor that has, in fact, kept him alive. His heart is well guarded and his soul protected from the villains who seek to unhorse him. Love, however, flows freely through the defense—for, without love and compassion, there is no purpose to his life, no reason for his journey, and no justification for his suffering. Love and the preservation of love are what give meaning to his existence.

The knight arrives at the break in the forest wall—there is nothing to be seen. The Moose, his questing beast, has once again disappeared into the mist. All that remains are the tell-tale signs of a magical presence. On a nearby tree, scrape marks upon the bark look to be the work of some large antlers! A tuft of hair beyond that! In the distance, there is a rustling in the vegetation—this is not the work of some wayward breeze! A trail unfolds before the warrior, and he must ride on. There will be no castles. No banquet halls. No courtly dances or kegs of ale. He has forsaken all of that, though all were freely offered. The knight has given himself over to God and to a cause much greater than all of that. Love and faith drive this lone knight errant, and love and faith protect him from the evils of a world that will never understand him. Let others seek joy and partake of the "finer things in life." There is something uniquely rewarding in traveling the spiritual path that leads to destinations unknown. There is something magical about believing and living in a dream that will not dissipate with the morning sun. The knight raises his sword and looks to Heaven. "For Valerie, for the Knight, for the Cause, and for God!"

In 1982, a dragon boat mysteriously emerged from the fog and drifted towards the shore where it settled. I was faced with a choice. I could either board the vessel and embark upon a voyage of unknown perils or I could allow the boat to simply drift away, receding back into the fog. I will never regret my decision, for the journey I have taken has been remarkably fulfilling; and the lessons I have garnered carry me yet through even the darkest days. I believe! I am grateful! And, from my heart—Thank you!

AFTERWORD

SO, WHERE'S THE HAPPY ENDING?

I humbly apologize for failing to provide a Hollywood style "riding off into the sunset" closing for my story. I love those endings, too. But this story isn't about the end. There's no dramatic finality as the curtains race together upon the stage. My story is about hope —it's a tale that continues so long as I draw breath upon this earth...maybe longer. Although I closed this memoir with a final tale from 2012, I might as well have closed with an ellipsis. Life is like that. All our glorious moments and all of our terrible failures quickly become "yesterdays," and what remains is today and tomorrow. I am eternally grateful for the many blessings I have known. But these great gifts are wasted unless I can carry the inspiration forward into tomorrow. And so I try, each and every day. Since 2012, I've seen my marriage break up and my children move thousands of miles away; I've retired from my life-long career as an Air Force officer, and I've attempted to navigate the challenges of a transition from military life to civilian life. I've been hired, and then I've been laid off; I've battled health issues and tried to comfort friends who were suffering through issues of their own. I've lost friends, but I've also made new friends. In short, I have lived. I have tried to live well. Biological processes provide me life; the inspiration and faith which I can trace back to 1982, and to Valerie, are what have allowed me to "live well." Despite the hardships, I continue to face each new day with hopeful enthusiasm and sincere gratitude. My faith is unbroken.

People sometimes ask if I am happy. It's a difficult question to answer. My short answer is "yes." I suspect the question isn't intended as the opening gambit to a lengthy philosophical discussion on the topic. However, I've always felt that happiness is a somewhat transitory state. Frankly, I'd be a little leery of someone who boasted that they were happy all the time. That seems unnatural. I'm not sure I'd want to be "happy" all the time. I'd miss out on a large chunk of "the human experience." I would certainly find it difficult to be empathetic. But I am a happy person. I smile when I see a flock of geese fly overhead; I sing aloud when the cool breeze and the clouded skies whisk my mind off to another place, another time. But, more important than these transitory moments of joy is an enduring sense of peace that has filled my heart these many years. It sustains me as I navigate the storms set before me. One finds true peace when expectations are put aside and you live in the present, appreciating all of the wonder that surrounds us. One finds true peace when you realize there is no one better to be in this world than yourself—your true self. When you live without pretense, without layering mask upon mask, then you live with integrity; you will find the confidence to defy the critiques of those who seek to marginalize you and the media onslaught that screams "you want to be like this man or that woman!" You don't. And you won't. When you live with integrity, you will withstand the incredible pressures to conform; you'll know that you owe no one an apology for being who you are. Be yourself. Period. I'm there. I will remain there. I owe it to Valerie and my Friends on high for giving me the strength to fight through the darkest days and, ultimately, instilling in me the confidence that I know will carry me through greater storms yet.

So, what, if any, takeaways would I hope you depart with? Here are a few thoughts:

1. Little things have meaning—you and I all have the ability to make a difference in someone's life just like Valerie made a difference in mine. A little bit of caring and the willingness to share some time with a stranger, or a friend, can be incredibly impactful. Please never forget this. I never have.

2. Do not be afraid to chase your crazy dreams. You might actually catch one.

3. Say "thank you" when you have a chance. Don't let that moment slip away. Life is too short—let people know that you love them and that you care about them...or even just that you respect them. Don't live regretting the words you failed to speak or the hug you failed to give.

4. Be yourself. It takes courage. You may have people poke fun at you, and you may feel isolated. The alternative is worse. Be who you are, not who someone else wants you to be.

In 1982 the foundations were laid for my very individual journey. I owe an incredible debt of gratitude to Valerie. Her kindness lives within me still, and she will always be part of who I am. I owe it to Lady Valerie to carry on and to try to make a difference in this world in whatever small way I can. It all starts with kindness.

PLEASE, PLEASE, PLEASE NEVER GIVE UP
- Life Is the Happy Ending -

EPILOGUE

Valerie Dudoward

*V*alerie Ruth Dudoward (Wilgoosg'm Neax, or "Wise Killer Whale") was born in Prince Rupert, British Columbia, Canada on February 6, 1957, at the Prince Rupert Regional Hospital, the daughter of James Albert Dudoward, Sr. and Ruth Amy Dudoward (Wan'm Neax). Descending from the Tsimshian Royal House of Waabs Mediik, she was, quite literally, a princess by lineage. Valerie grew up in a loving household along-side her younger siblings, Jim Dudoward, Jr., and sister, Pamela. Valerie's father was a hard-working and very successful fisherman who proudly named his boats after his daughters—the "Miss Valerie," honoring his oldest. Valerie's mother, Ruth, was a high-ranking Tsimshian matriarch and a respected elder.

From a very young age, Valerie's incredible intellect was apparent. Like many child prodigies, she was initially misunderstood by her elementary school teacher who actually suggested that she be placed into a special education program. It didn't take long for the school to realize the error—Valerie was recommended to be advanced two grades. To protect her daughter's youth, Valerie's mother wisely requested that Valerie be kept with her classmates.

At home, Valerie always maintained a special relationship with her siblings—serving as a nurturing and protective older sister. Those who knew her at a young age clearly recognized the natural kindness, sensitivity, and gentle disposition that remained a hall-mark of her life. These, combined with a keen intellect and an infectious sense of humor, helped make Valerie the kind of person who excelled in uplifting those around her.

Recognizing her academic excellence, Valerie was selected to represent Prince Rupert as a student contestant on the nationally broadcast *Reach For The Top* television show. She was also selected to participate in a Montreal Exchange Student Program. At the early age of 16, Valerie was hired, on a part-time basis, as a radio announcer/operator for CFPR Prince Rupert, becoming the first Aboriginal person to be hired at a Canadian Broadcasting Corporation (CBC) location. Her sister recounts, with pride, hearing her sister's voice on the radio and how Valerie would occasionally play special songs for her. Valerie worked with CBC until 1976 when she left for Vancouver, B.C. to create an Aboriginal radio program called *Talking Stick* and also created and launched a training program to train First Nations youth from all over British Columbia to become broadcasters, journalists, and researchers. The trainees would then return to their villages to develop local indigenous programming. Valerie also worked for a time as a television broadcaster in Terrance, B.C.

In 1974, Valerie became a reluctant Miss Prince Rupert Pageant winner. The idea of entering into a "beauty contest" was not in line with Valerie's feminist ideals; but after a bit of coaxing from friends and mentors, she realized the experience might provide her with a platform to voice concerns regarding important issues that were not being appropriately highlighted elsewhere. It was a golden opportunity to represent those without a voice—she might speak to the plight of First Nations people and the challenges facing Aboriginal youth and women, in particular. Besides winning the overall pageant (a first for a First Nations woman), Valerie also took first place in the talent competition with a flute-accompanied dramatic reading of a poem she wrote only the night before, in French and English. Following her victory, Valerie displayed the courage her friends and family knew well—she was a gentle spirit but was uncompromising when it came to her values. When the new pageant winner was asked to represent Prince Rupert in the Miss PNE Pageant, Valerie told the organizers that she wanted to wear traditional First Nations garb instead of the standard pageant gown during the PNE Parade and events. Organizers initially refused the request, but Valerie insisted upon it as a condition for her participation. The parade organizers capitulated, and Valerie participated in the parade...wearing a traditional First Nations leather dress and mukluks so that she could proudly represent all Northwest Coast First Nations peoples!

As previously mentioned, Valerie moved to Vancouver in 1976. With her incredible talent, intellect, and ever-growing resume of professional accomplishments, she could have easily basked in the limelight and pursued a high-paying career in the news or entertainment industry. Instead, Valerie chose a life of service, one where she might help others and give back to the community.

In Vancouver, Valerie created the first Aboriginal radio program, called *Talking Stick*, which was nationally broadcast across Canada. She also co-founded an Aboriginal newspaper, *Kahtou*, which is still in print today.

Throughout her life, Valerie was recognized as an accomplished writer, playwright, and poet. She was passionate about writing—a passion that began at a very young age. Her plays have been professionally staged in multiple venues in Canada; her plays and other writings have appeared in various anthologies, high school textbooks, and other publications. Valerie was also an award-winning host of a community cable program called *Pressure Point* which, again, shed light on many important community issues.

Valerie's career as a counselor, educator, and community spokesperson was incredibly impressive. She engaged in every conceivable manner, contributing to the betterment of indigenous communities within Canada. Her sister, Pamela, writes, "Her extensive career achievements and contributions within the government, corporate, the Urban Aboriginal Lower Mainland communities, educational institutes, the literary world, community organizations, and other professional affiliations are substantial and far too many to list." Pam goes on to write, "Her emphasis was always on helping people in very real and tangible ways as well as expressing herself artistically through her many talents and promoting her culture." Valerie's volunteer work included two years of service as the Provincial Women's Equity Representative to the BC Labour Force Development Board, co-founding the Aboriginal Personnel Employment Network, in addition to holding numerous board of directors, advisory boards, and committee positions.

Throughout her life, Valerie was an enthusiastic traveler. She loved learning about other cultures and was very aware that her experiences were helping her grow as a person. Travel was such a priority that Valerie sold her apartment to finance her European travel in 1982. This was a bold move, to be sure—Valerie was a bold person.

It's unfortunate that I do not have a more complete record of all the many community support and counseling jobs Valerie held over the years. When we met in 1990, she was already a veteran social worker and was currently working as a counselor for aboriginal youth navigating the challenges of integrating into an urban environment while not losing their cultural identity. For many years she worked with "First Nations Focus" in Vancouver as their Program Coordinator. She later worked the Choices program at the Helping Spirit Lodge. In 2006, Valerie was listed as being the Director of Aboriginal Education at Metropolitan College in Vancouver. Suffice it to say, Valerie gave as much of herself as anybody possibly could to support the people and the causes she believed in, and she did so with all of her heart.

The most difficult part of this short biography is the ending. Officially, Valerie Dudoward died of pneumonia on September 24, 2006. As one might imagine, there is more to the story. The full details will likely never be known. During an incredibly vulnerable period in her life, she found herself caught up in a terribly abusive relationship. She suffered physical and emotional abuse and was purposefully alienated from the friends and family members who truly loved her. As a woman who spent many years of her life working with abused First Nations women in similar circumstances, it may seem remarkable that Valerie was unable to extricate herself from this dark territory. This truly speaks to the unrelenting grip that perpetrators have on their victims—it is a tragedy of the worst kind. Had she been with friends, family, or even any decent person, it's very likely that a quick ambulance ride and appropriate medical attention would have saved Valerie's life. She received no medical attention. Her spirit left this world, free to travel into the next life, and free from the pain and sadness that characterized her final days.

In the wake of this terrible tragedy, the magnitude of the sadness and the greatness of the out-pouring of love were beyond measure. Horrible legal battles ensued between Valerie's loving family and the representatives of Valerie's dark-hearted former partner. While the nature of these engagements is outside the scope of this narrative, the end results should be noted. Valerie's remains were eventually properly honored as Tsimshian cultural protocols dictate. A court order allowed the family brief access to the apartment where she had been living with her partner so that a few items might be collected for the traditional burning cere-mony. Sadly, nearly all of Valerie's belongings, including her writ-ings, photographs, jewelry, clothing, and personal items were lost...forever. This is a great tragedy. What remains are the beau-tiful memories that no villain can steal from us.

Who was Valerie Dudoward? She was many things to many people. Like most of us, she was not without her faults and weak-nesses. But everyone I have ever spoken to about her unanimously agrees that she was a remarkable person. There was nothing superficial about Valerie—she was as real as they get. Valerie truly cared about people—she had great empathy and compassion. Valerie had a beautiful spirit, a loving heart, and a gentle disposition. She also possessed great courage. Valerie bravely stood up for the causes she believed in and supported those in need. And then there was her smile! Perhaps the loveliest I have ever seen. True, she was a great beauty...but she was never comfortable being identified as such. Her accomplishments were many, and they were very significant, but she was incredibly humble and rarely spoke about any of it. I had no idea of the great things she had done until after her passing. But I knew what Valerie needed me to know— that I had value and that she cared. I suspect many people who Valerie came across throughout the years might say the same thing. Valerie was not about self-promotion; she was about building up those in need. She left us too soon, but she left a beautiful legacy—all of us whose lives she touched. We will always remember her, and we'll be reminded that there is good in this world. This is a great gift. We owe it to Valerie to share the message.

ABOUT THE AUTHOR

Colonel David Lange grew up on Long Island, New York and received his commission as an officer in the United States Air Force in 1988, after graduating from the United States Air Force Academy. A decorated combat veteran, he flew numerous combat, combat support, and humanitarian relief missions during his career and was awarded the prestigious Institute of Navigation Superior Achievement Award in recognition of his life-long accomplishments as a practicing navigator. After completing two Master's degrees and holding a number of senior leadership positions, Colonel Lange retired from the Air Force in 2018, following

30 years of distinguished active duty military service, and returned home to New York. As a military officer, Colonel Lange authored several significant documents for the Department of Defense, contributed to a number of published articles, and served as an executive speech writer. During his lifetime, David has lived in ten states and two foreign countries and traveled to several dozen more foreign nations. Beyond sharing stories from his life, he is passionate about encouraging people to live authentically and appreciate all the things that make them unique and special. David shares a message of hope and gratitude and extols the importance of supporting each other to help make the world a better place for all of us and for future generations.